KINO AND THE WOMAN QUESTION

Kino and the Woman Question

Feminism and Soviet Silent Film

JUDITH MAYNE

Ohio State University Press, Columbus

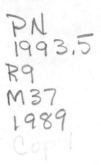

PN
1993.5
R9
M37
1989
Cop 1

Portions of chapter 2, 3, and 5 appeared, in an earlier version, in *Jump Cut,*
no. 23 (1980): 26–29. A previous version of chapter 6 appeared in *Ciné-tracts* 1
(1977): 81–91.

Library of Congress Cataloging-in-Publication Data

Mayne, Judith.
    Kino and the woman question : feminism and Soviet silent film /
Judith Mayne.
        p.   cm.
    Includes index.
    ISBN 0-8142-0481-3 (alk. paper)
        1. Motion pictures—Soviet Union—History.   2. Feminism and motion
pictures—Soviet Union.   3. Women in motion pictures.   4. Silent films.
5. Motion pictures—Philosophy.   I. Title.
PN1993.5.R9M37   1989
791.43'09'09352042—dc19   88-36622
                                                                    CIP

The paper in this book meets the guidelines for permanence and durability of
the Committee on Production Guidelines for Book Longevity of the Council on
Library Resources.

Printed in the U.S.A.

9 8 7 6 5 4 3 2 1

For Abdeslam Akkar and Marianne Cathelin

Contents

Acknowledgments   *ix*

Introduction   *1*

1. The Woman Question and Soviet Silent Film   *13*

2. *Strike* and Displaced Vision   *65*

3. *Mother* and Son   *91*

4. *Bed and Sofa* and the Edge of Domesticity   *110*

5. *Fragment of an Empire* and the Woman in the Window   *130*

6. *Man with a Movie Camera* and Woman's Work   *154*

Afterword   *184*

Notes   *193*

Index   *207*

Acknowledgments

I WOULD would like to thank my friends and colleagues who have assisted me in this project. My friendships with Abdeslam Akkar and Marianne Cathelin have sustained the writing of this book in challenging and productive ways. Noël Burch, who read early versions of several chapters, gave me both helpful criticism and encouragement. Vance Kepley and Tania Modleski offered wonderfully perceptive readings of the manuscript and excellent suggestions for how it could be improved. The Graduate School, the College of Humanities, the Department of Romance Languages and Literatures and the Center for Women's Studies at The Ohio State University have provided me with a pleasant place to work and with support in the form of grants and released time. The Ohio Arts Council supplied a Critic's grant which allowed me to complete this project. I am particularly grateful to Alex Holzman and Charlotte Dihoff of The Ohio State University Press for their patience, enthusiasm, and encouragement. Special thanks to Terry Moore for day-to-day support and comic relief.

Introduction

THIS BOOK explores a relatively short but extremely important period of the cinema, a period framed by Sergei Eisenstein's first feature film, *Strike* (1925), on the one hand, and on the other, by two films made in 1929 (Friedrich Ermler's *Fragment of an Empire* and Dziga Vertov's *Man with a Movie Camera*). I approach this period of film history, not in terms of the familiar tensions between art and politics, that is, between cinematic experimentation and socialist proselytizing,[1] but rather in terms of other, equally complex tensions concerning gender and sexual politics. During the decade of the 1920s, Soviet film emerged as a distinct style, based on the principles of dynamic tension, sharp contrast, rapid movement, and cinematic rhythm that have come to be associated with the theory and practice of montage. The five films to be discussed in detail in subsequent chapters—the three mentioned above as well as V. I. Pudovkin's *Mother* (1926) and Abram Room's *Bed and Sofa* (1927)—embody the most distinctive features of Soviet film practice. These films are evocative in another way as well; each reflects a major preoccupation with gender and sexual dichotomy. All of these films are, whether in an explicit or in a more implicit, even unconscious way, explorations of woman's position within socialist culture. My primary focus will be on how the narrative, aesthetic, and ideological projects of Soviet silent film are shaped, subverted, or otherwise complicated by representations of women.

After more than a decade of feminist film theory and criti-

1

cism, it has become almost as common, in film studies, to speak of sexual difference and the male gaze as it is to speak of reverse shots and close-ups. Feminist film theorists and critics have interrogated the most basic and fundamental aspects of the cinema, arguing, as Laura Mulvey did in her 1975 essay "Visual Pleasure and Narrative Cinema," that categories previously described as narrative and visual—point-of-view shots, for instance—are more appropriately described as categories of gender whereby, in Mulvey's words, men look and women are defined in terms of their "to-be-looked-at-ness."[2] The primary object of feminist film analysis has been that ubiquitous entity, the classical Hollywood cinema. The classical Hollywood cinema refers, roughly, to a period from the advent of sound film through the demise of the studio system and, more significantly, to a mode of filmmaking. The classical Hollywood cinema is more than a style, although it certainly comprises certain stylistic features, such as symmetrical uses of repetition and difference, "invisible" editing, and realist conventions. The classical Hollywood cinema is also—to use the language of contemporary film theory—an apparatus, an institution; that is, a system that encompasses a wide range of components, from modes of distribution and exhibition to modes of reception, and which engages a wide range of oppositions and tensions.[3]

To be sure, feminist critics are as interested in alternatives to the classical cinema as they are in inspecting, appropriating, or otherwise dismantling the components that make Hollywood films both engaging and ideologically complicit. With few exceptions, the feminist dialectic of the institution and its alternatives has been posed as follows: if woman is "other" in the classical Hollywood cinema, and if the cinema is a signifying system (that is, a network of coded elements, rather than a series of images which may or may not correspond to life outside the movie theater), then the most productive alternative will be to deconstruct the codes and conventions of the Hollywood cinema. Hence, alternative films are not necessarily those which replace a male point of view with a female one, but rather those which underscore the impossibility of the woman's position in traditional discourse, and the subsequent difficulty of any notion of "replacement."

A problem raised by current directions in feminist film theory and criticism is particularly relevant to this book.[4] The classical Hollywood cinema has become the norm against which all other alternative film practices are measured. Films which do not engage the classical Hollywood cinema are by and large relegated to irrelevance. Frequently, the very notion of an "alternative" is posed in the narrow terms of an either-or: either one is within classical discourse and therefore complicit, or one is critical of and/or resistant to it and therefore outside of it. To be sure, there are, in feminist film theory and criticism, impressive traditions of reading Hollywood films "against the grain," and of evaluating the ways in which female spectatorship—particularly in those films specifically intended for female audiences—complicates what has become common wisdom about the necessary links between the male subject and the classical cinema. Feminist theory and criticism thus have encouraged a more complex and contradictory view of the classical Hollywood cinema. But complexity and contradiction notwithstanding, the classical Hollywood cinema has retained its position as the norm against which all other cinemas are to be measured.

Soviet film of the 1920s raises other questions for feminist criticism. Some feminist critics have argued, for instance, that sexual difference is the primary, central opposition structuring the Hollywood cinema; indeed, that the classical cinema is, precisely, about the orchestration and dramatization of the founding moments of sexual identity—male sexual identity, specifically. Hence Kaja Silverman writes, for instance, that "dominant film practice orchestrates the burdensome transfer of male lack to the female subject by projecting the projections upon which our current notions of gender depend." That this orchestration of "male lack" is a function, not of the cinema in general, but rather of the classical cinema, is stressed by Silverman, who notes that "the displacement of losses suffered by the male subject onto the female subject is by no means a necessary extension of the screening situation. Rather, it is the effect of a specific scopic and narratological regime."[5] The films which I will examine in subsequent chapters are most definitely of a different "scopic and narratological regime" than the classical Hollywood cinema. My aim is to explore how the narrative and visual structures of Soviet films represent women. I will use rarely the phrase "sexual difference," which has come to refer not only to male and female polarity, but also to a preoccupation with questions of particular interest to psychoanalysis concerning lack, castration, and the production of meaning. This should not be construed as a rejection of the value of psychoanalysis as a critical perspective, nor as a mark of affiliation with the social, as opposed to the psychic—as if the two are ever so easily separable. Yet a reading of Soviet films as reenactments of castration anxiety, or as recreations of Oedipal scenarios, risks affirming, rather than challenging, the hegemony of the classical cinema. I see little value for feminism in assisting in the creation of a universal, transhistorical, transcultural male subject.

The context for this study is more appropriately described as the "woman question." The woman question is, of course, the classic Marxist formulation of the position of women.[6] As is well known, Freud's most famous formulation of the position of women within and for psychoanalysis was in the form of that infamous question, "What does a woman want?"[7] Thus the woman question evokes simultaneously Marxism and psychoanalysis, the registers of both social and psychic significance. I do not wish, however, to reactivate for feminist film criticism the fantasy of integration described by Roland Barthes:

How can the two great *epistemes* of modernity, namely the materialist and the Freudian dialectics, be made to intersect, to unite in the production of a new human relation (it is not to be excluded that a third term may be hidden in the inter-diction of the first two)? That is to say: how can we aid the inter-action of these two desires—to change the economy of the relations of production and to change the economy of the subject?[8]

Barthes's flirtation with a "third term" notwithstanding, the two desires evoked here presume "production" and the "sub-ject" to be self-evident categories, and as feminist analysis has demonstrated again and again, the self-evident is usually male. That the woman question slides between the registers of social and psychic significance and relevance I take, not as a badge of allegiance to the integration of Marxism and psycho-analysis, but rather as an indication of the fluid boundaries between woman as a psychic and as a social category.

By analyzing the representation of women in Soviet film of the 1920s, I am questioning whether there is a position for women in these films. A representation of woman is not the same thing as a position for women, and my feminist readings of these films are designed to raise questions about Soviet cinema which either have been unasked, marginalized, or repressed. Hence, I am attempting in the present study to extend the range of feminist film criticism beyond the scope of the classical Hollywood cinema. Now, one of the difficulties in reading Soviet films of the 1920s from a feminist perspec-tive is that the aesthetic and ideological projects of these films are so overdetermined by various trends and developments within film history and theory. Soviet filmmaking of the 1920s is best known for the theory and practice of montage. One classical view of montage comes from André Bazin, for whom montage was a manipulative form that detracted from the true vocation of the cinema, the re-creation of the ambiguity of the natural world. Hence montage was opposed to deep focus, the cinematic technique which epitomized, in Bazin's view, the destiny of the cinema, which was to give the spectator "a relation with the image closer to that which he enjoys with reality." Whereas montage, according to Bazin, "by its very nature rules out ambiguity of expression, . . . depth of focus reintroduced ambiguity into the structure of the image if not of necessity—Wyler's films are never ambiguous—at least as a possibility."[9]

Bazin's assumptions about the nature of cinema have been criticized on virtually every front by the practitioners of contemporary film theory, and in particular by those critics associated with the development of film theory in France in the 1970s. Jean-Louis Comolli, for example, rejected Bazin's claims about the cinema as idealist and essentialist, and turned the opposition of deep focus and montage on its head.[10] If deep focus was redefined as potentially quite manipulative in its own right, montage would be seen as having the potential to draw attention to the processes of cinematic production, thereby creating an active, dynamic position for the spectator. And since the relationship between Marxism and avant-garde practice was a topic of discussion in such influential journals as *Tel Quel,* interest in Soviet films of the 1920s was rekindled. To be sure, Soviet films of the 1920s meant different things to different people, but a common theme was the concept of montage as a radical subversion of the relationship between reality and representation, between figure and diegesis. As Marie-Claire Ropars puts it in her analysis of Eisenstein's *October,* montage defines reality as the "result of an inquiry and not as a given: it is through the production of meaning that one comprehends the world, not in the reproduction of appearances . . ."[11]

In more recent years, there has been a shift in film studies away from the sweeping generalizations concerning ideology, dominant discourse, and signifying practice that characterized much writing about the cinema in the early 1970s. In the process, Soviet film of the 1920s not only has been discussed less frequently in such a polemic way, but discussed less frequently, period. The shift in contemporary film studies is not necessarily a movement away from a preoccupation with ideology, but rather, an exploration of different concepts of ideology and of the different levels on which ideology works. That shift is evidenced by the increasing visibility of the word "history" in film studies. If, a decade or so ago, the "ideological subject" was a major preoccupation in film studies, the "historical subject" is a more appropriate depiction of current concerns. Ideology and history are not mutually exclusive, of course, but there is now a tendency in film studies to put the theoretical claims of the previous decade to the test of history. A comparable, if more subtle, change is evidenced in the scope of detailed readings of individual films. These appear to be less concerned with how a single film demonstrates, say, the dominant features of the norm of the classical Hollywood cinema, and more preoccupied with how a film exceeds or is otherwise irreducible to a set of codes. As a result, of course, the very notion of a "norm" has become considerably more problematic.

In *Narration and the Fiction Film,* David Bordwell discusses the "historical-materialist" mode of film narration, the name he gives to the style of film narrative developed in Soviet films of the 1920s. In his analysis of historical-materialist narration, Bordwell posits montage, and the modes of spectatorship associated with it, in terms quite different from either the Bazinian position or the more recent approach. Hence, Bordwell speaks of an:

idiosyncratic approach to the spectator, one that is neither as 'total-itarian' as liberal-humanist critics often assume nor as radical as some recent theorists of textuality have claimed. The films' mixture of didactic and poetic structures calls for viewing procedures which deviate from classical norms yet remain unified by protocols specific to this mode.

For Bordwell, the self-conscious narration of Soviet film exists alongside a strong allegiance to a political signified; in other words, the experimental form of the films really does not put into question the coherence of their address. Narration tends, says Bordwell, to be "constantly overt, but it seldom creates connotative ambiguity."[12]

What I find most interesting in Bordwell's account, aside from its reassessment of critical views of Soviet film, is the notion of ambiguity. Bazin's criticism of montage was based on its refusal of ambiguity in favor of overt manipulation. For the "theorists of textuality" to whom Bordwell refers—Jean-Louis Comolli and Jean Narboni, for instance—montage functioned, rather, as a most ambiguous technique. But "ambiguity" here has a meaning altogether different from the notion of an ambiguous reality central to Bazin's view. Rather, from this point of view, montage is ambiguous in the sense that it engages a multiplicity of possible meanings and readings, and thus anticipates a separation between signifier and signified. In other words, montage represents a challenge to the coherence of the political register, for which a seamless fit between signifier and signified is necessary. Bordwell suggests that for these theorists of textuality, there is a confusion between overt narration and "connotative ambiguity."

While I share Bordwell's scepticism about both the total-itarian and radical claims that have been made for Soviet film narrative, I will argue nonetheless that ambiguity is quite often present in Soviet film narrative. However many different positions there are on Soviet film, they share a notion of the fundamental political coherence of the films in question. For Bazin, political coherence is precisely what makes the films less "cinematic." For theorists of the 1970s, political coherence is a somewhat more complex issue—or more confusing, depending on your point of view. Here, political relevance is defined, not in the traditional sense of an allegiance to a political signified, but rather in terms of a commitment to textual process and self-conscious representation. Bordwell argues that the self-conscious, or overt, narration, which these critics have taken to be a symptom of the thoroughly radical formal process of Soviet films, does not in any way compromise political coherence.

When Soviet films are examined in terms of the representation of women and the attendant issues of gender, the question of political coherence is posed differently. Indeed, examination of the woman question in Soviet film suggests that political coherence is a problematic entity; the woman question foregrounds crucial tensions that inform the films on many levels. These include not only the obvious tensions between men and women, and the public and the private, that one might expect. There are other tensions that are not necessarily reducible to a gender dynamic, such as the relationship between class struggle as a fundamental principle of Soviet film and other seemingly secondary issues which are ostensibly subordinate, but which may complicate political coherence rather than support it. I suggest that ambiguity be defined neither in the Bazinian sense of a transcendental reality, nor in the sense of an *écriture* that assumes a radical status by virtue of challenging the cinematic codes of linear continuity and realism. I read these films, rather, as ambiguous in the sense that they illuminate the contradictions that are inevitable when the development of an art form, and particularly a nascent art form such as the cinema, is intertwined with an ideological agenda and with social transformation. Nowhere are those contradictions more evident than in Soviet cinematic explorations of the woman question. In other words, the cinematic ways in which the woman question is posed exemplify the ambiguity characteristic of Soviet film narrative.

The films which will be discussed in subsequent chapters are, for the most part, the classics of the 1920s. My concern is less with recreating and recomposing the cinematic landscape of the 1920s, than with rereading the films which have become a part of the institution of film history and film theory. Some of the films, such as *Bed and Sofa* and *Fragment of an Empire,* are less well known than others. But there are no discoveries of previously ignored films to be found here. Nor do I attempt to seek compensatory treatment for the women directors who have been ignored or marginalized in film history, women such as Olga Preobrazhenskaya and Esther Shub.[13] The only theoretical justification I offer for the fact that all of the directors whose films I shall examine are male is that the scope of my study is defined by Soviet film of the 1920s as an already constituted field. Examination of the works of women filmmakers of the 1920s might offer evidence of a radical difference, that is, of other approaches to filmmaking which would challenge the standard views of and assumptions about the time. My concern, however, is with "difference" understood in another, and admittedly more narrow sense: a difference in reading, a difference in interpretation, of Soviet film classics of the 1920s. Teresa DeLauretis defines the goal of feminist criticism as a questioning of the relationship between "woman" and "women." "Woman," for DeLauretis, refers to a "fictional construct," "sign and object of men's social exchange," the "vanishing point of our culture's fictions of itself and the condition of the discourses in which the fictions are represented." "Women" are "the real historical beings who cannot as yet be defined outside of those discursive formations."[14] In these terms, the present project is an analysis of "woman" in Soviet films of the 1920s from the vantage point of a "women's" perspective shaped and defined by contemporary feminist theory and criticism.

My readings of individual films take the form of textual analyses, that is, examinations not only of the dominant structures of the individual text, but also and especially of what escapes, exceeds, or otherwise complicates those dominant structures. Feminist textual analysis has a vested interest in reading critically the central concepts that have informed the theory and practice of textual analysis. For instance, a central assumption of structuralist analysis is that the text is governed by patterns of binary opposition. But the notion of opposition often conceals a hierarchy whereby one term is privileged over the other. Obviously gender oppositions are of key importance, but the question is also one of a mode of representation where difference and hierarchy collide. Given the central importance of montage in Soviet silent film, I will devote particular attention to how the techniques of montage, especially with their emphasis on sharp contrast and rapid movement, create remarkable collisions of difference and hierarchy.

I begin, in chapter one, with a discussion of the intersection of cinema and the woman question in the Soviet Union of the 1920s. In order to suggest, in a preliminary way, the cinematic contours of the woman question, I discuss four films. In Eisenstein's *Potemkin* (1925), the articulation of montage relies on an opposition between the abstract and the concrete, an opposition which quickly acquires the contours of gender. Lev Kuleshov's *By the Law* (1926) demonstrates how, in the adaptation of a literary source to the screen (Jack London's short story "The Unexpected"), the figure of woman emerges as the problematic link between past and present. In Eisenstein's *October*, the myth of the October Revolution relies crucially on the opposition between activity and passivity, and as with the tension between the abstract and the concrete in *Potemkin,* women are problematic figures in the negotiation of the opposition. *October* also turns on the relationship between nature and culture, which is the central theme of Alexander Dovzhenko's *Earth* (1930). In *Earth,* the figure of the woman emerges to complicate the absolute duality of socialism and capitalism so central to the film.

In subsequent chapters, I discuss in detail individual films, expanding upon the preliminary analyses in chapter one. In chapter two, I analyze the similar function of women and spies in Eisenstein's first feature film, *Strike* (1925). Chapter three focuses on Pudovkin's *Mother* (1926) as a film that can barely sustain its ostensible central focus on a woman. In chapter four, I examine the relationship between private and public life in Room's 1927 film *Bed and Sofa.* Chapter five is an analysis of Ermler's *Fragment of an Empire* (1929), in which the processes of memory and socialization depend upon a woman's function as both central to and external to socialist collectivity. Finally, in chapter six, I read Vertov's *Man with a Movie Camera* in terms of the issues of gender that are raised in this remarkably complex and innovative exploration of the relationship between production and filmmaking, and between the various activities that comprise the collective life of socialist society.

I make no claims as to the exhaustiveness of this study; I am less concerned with numbers of examples than with the intricacies of narrative and visual structure. Nonetheless, I have attempted, within a framework that is inevitably shaped by my own likes and preferences, to be fairly representative in my selection of films. These films reflect preoccupations common to many Soviet films of the period—the primacy of the class struggle and the positive achievements of socialism, on a thematic level, and the importance of montage as an aesthetic and ideological device. In these films, the woman question is a vantage point on the complex issues raised in Soviet silent film, as well as a forceful question in its own right.

1. The Woman Question and Soviet Silent Film

VIRTUALLY ALL critics of Soviet 1920s film would agree that the development of the cinema needs to be situated within the context of turbulent socialist change. Most frequently, this context is explained from the top down; that is, in terms of what the cinema represented for the Bolshevik agents of revolutionary change. According to Richard Taylor, "[t]he Bolsheviks needed to use propaganda and they chose the cinema as their principal weapon in the campaign to win the minds of the masses."[1] Hence, Soviet film is examined as an indication of the changing political dimensions of the Bolshevik regime.[2] To be sure, there is an enormous difference of focus depending on whether one is interested in Soviet film as one aspect of the development of socialism, or as one of the most significant chapters in the history of film. Yet the top-down approach characterizes many studies of Soviet film devoted primarily to aesthetic and narrative structures. Jay Leyda's *Kino: A History of the Russian and Soviet Film* documents the development of Soviet film art, in part by exploring the ways in which artistic and political desires intersected and collided. Even Bordwell, in his analysis of "historical-materialist narration," suggests that the "omnipotent" narration of Soviet montage films constitutes an appeal to an already constituted body of assumptions, a kind of political master code. Writing of Eisenstein's *Potemkin,* for instance, Bordwell says:

13

"The end of *Potemkin* neglects to mention that the rebelling sailors were eventually captured, but the viewer is supposed to understand that whatever the outcome of this episode, the entire 1905 revolution was a harbinger of 1917."[3]

While no one would dispute the crucial importance of historical and political context in a discussion of Soviet film, the context usually evoked tends to conform to a rather narrow definition of politics, having to do with official policy and the events that have become part of standard histories of the time. Rarely have the changes that occurred in the lives of women— with attendant implications for Soviet culture as a whole, grappling with new definitions of private and public spheres—been evoked in relation to the cinema. Many of the issues that are central to a contemporary feminist political agenda were raised during the early years of the Soviet socialist government. Sheila Rowbotham, for example, has said of the years immediately following the revolution that "[t]here has probably never been a time when great masses of people discussed openly questions which affected women so much."[4] Yet most discussions of Soviet cinema would lead one to believe that the wide-sweeping changes and challenges initiated by socialism had cinematic repercussions measurable only in terms of an industry shaped by a political program, of an ideological aesthetic based on the principles of montage, and of a narrative structure informed by a class dynamic understood in the narrowest sense.

While conpensatory treatment would be reason enough to consider the dynamics of gender in Soviet film in the 1920s, there are other reasons as well. The fate of the woman question in the Soviet Union was not unlike the fate of what might be referred to as the "cinema question." If the years 1928–29 (when bureaucratic scrutiny of the arts, through organizations like RAPP, the Russian Association of Proletarian Writers, became firmly entrenched) marked a closing-down of cinematic experimentation, they marked as well a rather decisive end to dialogue concerning the status of sexual politics within socialism.[5] To be sure, the latter years of the decade were to prove disastrous from many points of view; there was nothing particularly unique about women or the cinema in this respect. However, both questions—of woman and of the cinema—rely on a complex and often confusing mixture of tradition and change. In sexual terms, the mixture of tradition and change pitted women's social and historic status as men's servants against the presumption of equality amongst workers as a central tenet of socialist change.[6] In cinematic terms, the tension between tradition and change raises issues of narrative, and particularly of the relationship between conventional narrative forms and radical cinematic experimentation. I will argue that examination of how the woman question is posed in films of the 1920s offers a critical vantage point from which to comprehend the narrative strategies central to the development of Soviet cinema; and, similarly, that these narrative strategies are central to an understanding of the representation of women in relation to cultural and political change. In other words, I am encouraging a dialogue between the woman question and cinematic narrative. Such a dialogue involves an exploration of how Soviet film narrative turns, ideologically and aesthetically, on the representation of woman, and of how the woman question is concerned, centrally and vitally, with questions of narrative. In Soviet film of the 1920s, the possibilities for such a dialogue are rich indeed.

The development of Soviet film during the period of the 1920s occurs within a broader context in which various formulations of the relationship between art and politics were pursued with great verve and enthusiasm. Indeed, one of the most intriguing aspects of art and culture in the Soviet Union, post-1917 and pre-1929, is the role of experimentation and pluralism. To be sure, there was always, in the decade of the

1920s, some standard of political correctness to which different groups and individuals aspired. But the sheer number of competing ideologies suggested that the very formulation of the connection between art and politics was open to question. Now the pluralism that characterized the 1920s might be seen, somewhat pessimistically, as little more than confusion, which was eventually resolved by the imposition of artistic formulae, particularly through the efforts of Andrei Zhdanov. His name became virtually synonymous with the rigid requirements of socialist realism. Artistic pluralism thus was abolished in the name of Zhdanovian socialist realism. However, it seems more to the point, and certainly more useful for a consideration of film and ideology, to resist the temptation to see the 1920s as a simple rehearsal for what was to come. The period might be seen better as a challenge, a questioning, a working-through of what it means to talk about socialist art and culture in the first place.

There is, perhaps, no art form which better characterizes this multi-faceted socialist culture than film. Film was a new technological art form unencumbered by years of tradition, such as that of literature and the theater. The potential of film as both art form and pedagogical tool was recognized immediately. Film was seen as a valuable weapon in literacy campaigns, since images and written titles could aid in the acquisition of reading skills, as well as in the provision of politically instructive images and stories. Thus the cinema represented, for the Soviets, a new art form capable of responding to the demands of a new society. At the same time, this new art form was perceived as a means of providing continuity with the art and culture of the past. Leyda reports that in 1918, for example, scenario contests were sponsored by newly formed cinema committees: contestants were to submit scenarios for film adaptations of Turgenev's work to celebrate the 100th anniversary of the novelist's birth.[7]

Film was thus a new socialist art form, and a link to the prerevolutionary cultural past. It comes as no surprise that the cinema was expected to embody socialist change, but the formal experimentation central to many films of the 1920s was not always warmly received. The relationship of film to the traditions of the past was also a controversial issue. The relation of Soviet cinema to a narrative tradition is one specific instance of a much broader question in Soviet culture, one which is fundamental to an understanding of the pluralism of the 1920s: How are the arts to be understood dialectically in relationship to the past, and to a tradition that is predominantly middle-class? Should socialist culture strive to make a radical break with forms inherited from the past; or, rather, should socialism aim at making the culture of the past available to greater numbers of people? The two functions of the cinema—as a radical new form and as a means to revision and appropriate the past—were not necessarily integrated in the minds of filmmakers. Indeed, I would argue that whatever the claims of Soviet filmmakers, their films tended to be informed by a tension between these two functions. On the one hand, Soviet filmmakers would explore new directions in cinematic representation, concerning in particular the possibilities of montage. On the other, filmmakers would tap traditional narrative sources, either directly through adaptations, or indirectly through the more general devices of characterization, or narrative conflict and resolution. The differing views of Eisenstein and Vertov concerning the future of revolutionary cinema are relevant here. I am referring less to the difference between Eisenstein as defender of the fiction film versus Vertov as spokesperson for the documentary, than to their differences concerning, precisely, the nature of a dialectical approach to cinema. Eisenstein often spoke of elements of the literary tradition which were appropriated, in his films, to socialist ends. Thus he described the creation of a "mass hero" in *Strike* as opposed to the individual hero of bourgeois art; and he explained in detail that the creation of conflict in *Potemkin* occurs along the same lines as in the five-part structure of a classical tragedy.[8] Vertov insisted, however, that a socialist camera must turn away from all trappings of bourgeois art, and devote itself instead to the "exploration of the phenomena of life."[9]

For Eisenstein, the possibilities of cinematic representation had been suggested in middle-class art, and the goal of Soviet filmmakers was to realize those possibilities. Thus, montage in the cinema of D. W. Griffith suggested great potential, but it was only the experience of Soviet cinema that would allow the full potential of montage, as the fusion of technique and ideological consciousness, to be realized. Editing patterns in the films of D. W. Griffith were bound, according to Eisenstein, by ideological limitations:

And, naturally, the montage concept of Griffith, as a primarily parallel montage, appears to be a copy of his dualistic picture of the world, running in two parallel lines of poor and rich towards some hypothetical 'reconciliation' where ... the parallel lines would cross, that is, in that infinity, just as inaccessible as that 'reconciliation.'[10]

Even in the hands of a brilliant technician like Griffith, montage is determined by the social imagination: "The structure that is reflected . . . is the structure of bourgeois society."[11]

For Vertov, it was also the function of Soviet filmmaking to realize the full potential of cinematic representation. However, there are no intermediate figures like Griffith in Vertov's view, figures who function as elements in a contradictory process, pointing to socialist possibilities while remaining ensconced in a capitalist view of the world. For Vertov, cinema in capitalist society always would be an instrument of distortion. Only when the technological advances of capitalist society are freed from the social conditions of capitalism will their real capacities be emancipated:

. . . the camera experienced a misfortune. It was invented at a time when there was no single country in which capital was not in power. The bourgeoisie's hellish idea consisted of using the new toy to entertain the masses, or rather to divert the workers' attention from their basic aim: the struggle against their masters.[12]

Put another way, Eisenstein's approach focuses on the potentially revolutionary elements in bourgeois culture; it is a dialectics of appropriation. Vertov, however, insists upon sharp breaks between bourgeois and socialist culture; his is a dialectics of emancipation. Both of these positions, in a variety of forms, are taken up in film narrative of the 1920s. Principles of appropriation may seem to be more in evidence, but the formal experimentation by many Soviet filmmakers, not just Vertov, suggests genuine and radical breaks with traditional or conventional forms.[13] While Eisenstein may initially appear to be much closer to the Leninist position, which argues for the socialist appropriation of traditions of the past, Lenin's encouragement of documentary film as a uniquely socialist enterprise suggests a view close to that of Vertov. In other words, the dividing lines between appropriation and emancipation are not always clearly defined.

The decade of the 1920s was characterized, in short, by a complex evaluation of the possibilities of narrative, and of the adaptation of established narrative forms to socialist purposes. Whether individual heroes, realist constructions, quest structures, and the like constituted, in and of themselves, middle-class and therefore problematic forms was open to question. There was a wide spectrum of possibilities open to narrative cinema. Traditional narrative elements might be transposed, quite simply, to socialist terms, thereby working from the assumption that form is subsidiary to the demands of socialist content. Or, those elements might be transformed, read against the grain, as it were, to subvert the ends they originally served. Finally, any narrative forms identified with Western middle-class culture might be rejected outright. When the options are described in this way, they conform to what has become common wisdom concerning the ascending scale of radicalism among Soviet filmmakers of the 1920s, with Pudovkin transposing traditional forms, Eisenstein transforming and reworking them, and Vertov rejecting them outright. I will argue, however, that the tension between appropriation and emancipation informs many films of the period, despite their apparent position in one camp versus another.[14] I will argue, as well, that the tension between appropriation and emancipation is particularly relevant to cinematic versions of the woman question. Soviet representations of women in films of the 1920s occupy an often precarious balance between stereotypically patriarchal, one-dimensional images of women (patriarchal here is not synonymous with middle-class; many socialist images are equally patriarchal) and contradictory figures that expose tensions and do not neatly serve narrative or ideological demands for unity and coherence. While the class component is clearly central, the tension I am describing cannot be put adequately as an opposition of "middle-class" versus "socialist" views. Nor can it be described as a tension between male and female points of view. In the films to be discussed here, the subject of the narrative—whether acknowledged or unacknowledged—is male, even though some of the films explore, briefly and momentarily for the most part, a female point of view. Rather, this is a tension between representations that project male-centered fantasies, and representations that undermine, rather than affirm, a male-centered viewpoint. For some Soviet filmmakers, traditional images of women were appropriated along with traditional narrative forms; for others, the emancipatory goal of cinema included a gender component. But more important, cinematic representations of women offer a vantage point from which to read critically the strategies of both appropriation and emancipation, and to question the extent to which Soviet film narrative maintains, or puts into question, the centrality of the male subject.

There is a particular fit between narrative and gender, in part because storytelling casts binary oppositions into complex networks, and in part because, traditionally and historically, narrative has served both to reinforce the male subject as center of the universe, and to contest that centrality with distinctly female-centered narratives. Lenin's observations on novelists and novel writing are instructive in this regard. The Bolshevik leader's fondness for Tolstoy is well known, and suggests that in a dialectically informed culture, bourgeois art would be made available for all to appreciate.

Tolstoy the artist is known to an infinitesmal minority even in Russia. If his great works are really to be made the possession of all, a struggle must be waged against the system of society which condemns millions and scores of millions to ignorance, benightedness, drudgery and poverty—a socialist revolution must be accomplished.

Tolstoy . . . produced artistic works which will always be appreciated and read by the masses, once they have created human conditions of life for themselves after overthrowing the yoke of the landlords and capitalists . . .

Tolstoy's greatness, for Lenin, resides in the novelist's accurate depictions of the contradictions of the prerevolutionary era.

Belonging, as he did, primarily to the era of 1861–1904, Tolstoy in his works—both as an artist and as a thinker and preacher—embodied in amazingly bold relief the specific historical features of the entire first Russian revolution, its strength and its weakness.[15]

Although he is referring here to Tolstoy's particular contribution within a particular period of history, Lenin describes what is a fundamental feature of most traditional narratives, the creation of a social universe. In this respect, Lenin's attention to Tolstoy mirrors what would become a central concern of those filmmakers who, similarly, regarded the cinema as a means of creating in "amazingly bold relief" a social universe of socialism.

Lenin's admiration for Tolstoy was matched only by his praise for the nineteenth-century author Nikolai Chernyshevsky, whose 1864 novel *What Is To Be Done?* provided the title for Lenin's early collection of essays (1902) on the role of the party in revolutionary struggle.[16] Lenin adopted the title in homage to Chernyshevsky, and he described the author as one of the most profound influences on his development as a Marxist. Lenin said that *What Is To Be Done?* caused a revolution in his own thought, and prepared him for reading Marx.[17] "The spirit of class struggle flows through all [Chernyshevsky's] works," said Lenin, and he described Chernyshevsky as a "socialist utopian who dreamt of the transition to socialism through the old, semi-feudal commune . . ."[18]

Chernyshevsky's *What Is To Be Done?* is subtitled "Tales about New People." In the novel, male and female characters representing different philosophical positions experiment with alternative living situations. Based on the nature of Lenin's *What Is To Be Done?* one might expect the Chernyshevsky novel to deal with the same kind of "specific historical features," although of an earlier period, that Lenin so admired in Tolstoy. Most accounts of Chernyshevsky's influence on Lenin stress the novelist's role as socialist mentor, who introduced Lenin to the basic principles of socialist thought. Given the strategic importance of *What Is To Be Done?* one imagines perhaps a novel about peasant revolt, or about exploitation at the workplace. Yet Chernyshevsky's novel is, primarily, an exploration of sexual politics. The central female character of the novel, Vera Pavlovna, insists that her marriage be founded upon friendship. She and her husband live in separate rooms and lead independent lives.[19]

If the centrality of sexual politics in Chernyshevsky's novel has not been seen as particularly important in Lenin's development, there is another socialist on whom Chernyshevsky's influence has been cast in precisely those terms. It has been said that Inessa Armand, a woman revolutionary who was (apparently falsely) reputed to have been Lenin's lover, also was influenced by the author.[20] Legend has it that once she read Chernyshevsky's novel, Armand began to model herself on the character of Vera Pavlovna.[21] The influence of Chernyshevsky's *What Is To Be Done?* on these two particular revolutionaries corresponds to the two separate spheres of male and female, political and personal existence: there is the general political formation of Lenin, on the one hand, concerning the ideas of socialism, the "preparation" for Marx; and on the other, there is the personal formation of Armand. While Lenin's identification with Chernyshevsky takes the properly distanced form of a quotation, an homage, Armand's identification expresses itself in her merging with a fictional character. It is as if the sexual politics so central to Chernyshevsky's novel are speakable only in terms of one best known as an activist for women's rights (Armand served briefly as head of the Zhenotdel, the women's department, before her death in 1920), as a *woman* revolutionary; while the Lenin influenced by Chernyshevsky is, quite simply, a revolutionary. The novelist so respected by Lenin thus exists primarily as a social analyst, a theorist of the public sphere, while the considerations of private life and alternative living situations central to *What Is To Be Done?* are marginalized. The gesture whereby Lenin quotes Chernyshevsky in his 1902 title suggests, initially, a possibility of the convergence of two kinds of social analysis: that of the novel and that of the essay. Yet, at the same time, there is a repression of any connection between social analysis and the concerns of private life.

Along the same lines, a comment by Lenin later reported by Armand suggests a sharp separation between material appropriate for political pamphlets and that for novels. Lenin criticized a pamphlet Armand was preparing on free love.

In your pamphlet you have a juxtaposition not of class types, but something in the nature of "an individual case," which is possible, of course. But is this a question of individual cases? The theme of a separate, individual case of dirty kisses in marriage and pure kisses in a short-lived love affair should be developed in a novel (for here the whole point would be in the individual setting, in analysing the characters and psychology of given types). But in a pamphlet?[22]

Lenin criticizes the "individual case," but it is obvious that he objects as well to a discussion of personal life in a political pamphlet. In the contrast between novel and pamphlet, there are two kinds of political expression: the "individual" (or, the personal), and the "class types" (or, "genuine" political analysis).

Lenin's comments to Armand seem to represent what is repressed in his admiration for Chernyshevsky. Admiration for the nineteenth-century novelist disengages political analysis from the considerations of personal life pursued in Chernyshevsky's novel. And in Lenin's critique of Armand's approach to pamphlet writing, he finds the subject of "free love" more compatible with the novel form. Lenin's misgivings about "free love," personal life, and sexual politics are not simply a reflection of his rather well-known conservative views on such questions. Lenin's comments suggest, as well, the extreme difficulty of the very question of personal issues for the Soviets—that is, a difficulty of position, of placement, of knowing where, on the political spectrum, such issues belong. Lenin says that an exploration of the individual case would be more appropriate in a novel, that is, in a fictional narrative. But in film—the narrative form so emblematic of Soviet socialist society—the status of the personal, and of the relationship between the private and the public, also was a point of tension. Lenin's misgivings are not simply those of a political leader, for they suggest the potentially complex function of narrative in socialist society. The bureaucratic controls enforced by the end of the decade of the 1920s resolved the complexity by banishing any ambivalence to the realm of formalism and political incorrectness. In Soviet film of the 1920s, however, these tensions and conflicts are very much in evidence, even if they sometimes appear in somewhat submerged form. One of the most significant social functions of narrative is exploration of the relationship between the individual and the social, between the private and the public.[23] In a society where the very foundations of those relationships were being rethought and reformulated, one expects that the ideological function of narrative was, at the very least, contradictory.

Indeed, on the spectrum of concerns appropriate to novel versus pamphlet, where would Lenin place the cinema, which several years later he would qualify as the most important of the arts in the Soviet Union?[24] We know that Lenin was interested in the use of cinema in the literacy campaigns of the time, and that he encouraged the development of documentary film. The notion of the "Leninist Proportion" was meant to establish a definite ratio in film programs between fiction and documentary film.[25] Yet, even though Vertov would insist that the genuine Leninist position militated against the intrusion of narrative and theatrical elements into the "communist decoding of the world," the cinema envisaged by Lenin would seem to lie somewhere in between these poles represented by novel and pamphlet. For Soviet film was defined early in its revolutionary history as a unique hybrid of fiction and historical exposition. Films did not have quite the direct instrumental function of pamphlets, yet, because they were seen in social settings, they were defined more immediately in terms of public space than other art forms, such as the novel. Even if novels are read in private, they embody social panoramas; in fact, the very connection between fiction and history that is so central to Soviet film narrative was created by accentuating the capacity of narrative to create a public sphere.

In suggesting that there is a connection to be made between the debates on the status of women and the evolution of the Soviet narrative film in the 1920s, I do not mean to claim that there is some kind of cause and effect, linear relationship between the two domains. To be sure, there are some films which reflect, in very concrete terms, the controversy over what the new men and women of socialist society would be and how they would interact. However, I would stress that the woman question for cinema is much broader than a selection of films dealing literally and deliberately with the woman question as a specialized topic. Within the particular contours of cinematic narrative as they developed in the Soviet Union in the 1920s, woman is a figure that embodies the tensions I have described. I use the word "figure" in order to emphasize the necessarily figural as well as figurative dimension of these representations—figural in the sense that these representations of women are highly coded components in a visual and narrative system, and figurative in the sense that they are projections which, while not detached absolutely from the real women who populated Soviet society and consumed its myths, are nonetheless not reducible to real flesh and blood women. "Figure" thus emphasizes how representations of women are points of tension within Soviet film narrative. I do not, however, use the term in order to evoke the classic distinction between figure and diegesis, for I do not find it particularly useful (or, in many instances, even possible) to separate stylistic flourishes or rhetorical devices from the more immediate fictional world of the film.

For Marxism, as for psychoanalysis, the position of the woman is posed as a question, and if psychoanalysis has not always been entirely successful in understanding what a woman wants, neither has Marxism. The classic Marxist position is that the emancipation of women will occur with the abolition of private property and the full integration of women into the labor force. That such projections into a utopian future are problematic became obvious in the decade following the 1917 Revolution. The steps deemed necessary to build socialism—protection of the family as an economic unit, particularly in rural areas, and the free market established by the New Economic Policy, for instance —conflicted with measures that immediately would have improved the status of women. And there was the further problem of the traditional status quo in Russia, where women quite often were perceived as property in terms far more difficult to challenge than bourgeois ownership of the factories. Yet, within nineteenth-century socialism, there had been strong support for women's rights, and there was in Russia a strong feminist movement.[26] In the years immediately following the revolution, equality for women was on the Bolshevik agenda. After the Revolution of February 1917, women were granted full civil and political rights. "Granted" can be somewhat misleading, however. While it is true that women rarely occupied positions of leadership within the Bolshevik government, women were nonetheless significantly present in the struggles which led to the Bolsheviks' rise to power.[27] The first strike with which the provisional government of Kerensky had to contend was a strike of women laundry workers.[28]

That the Bolshevik regime was committed to female equality is suggested by the new marriage and family laws, introduced in 1917 and 1918, whereby women could initiate divorce and receive alimony; fathers (married or not) were made responsible for a child's support; marriage became a simple civil declaration; and couples were permitted to choose a surname. While the legislation is important, its existence does not reflect the conflicts and tensions that informed discussion of women and the family. The most insistent spokesperson for women's equality in the Soviet Union was undoubtedly Alexandra Kollontai. Even though she participated in drafting the Family Code, the final document was very much a compromise between Kollontai's views, which were aimed toward the eventual abolition of the nuclear family, and those of Lenin, which tended to be much more conservative.[29]

While the Bolshevik government was committed on paper to equality for women, the pressure of practical concerns took its toll. The institution of limited capitalist development, with the New Economic Policy (NEP) in 1921, was extremely detrimental to women. According to Kollontai, NEP constituted a "new threat," because 70 percent of the initial cutbacks involved women.[30] The marriage laws, while quite attractive on paper, did not account sufficiently for the different status of men and women. Hence, many women became victims of the new marriage laws. Abandoned by their spouses and unable to support their children, many took to prostitution.[31] While the Communist party did initiate a women's department, the Zhenotdel, it was virtually always the subject of controversy. The term "feminism" suggested separatism to the Bolsheviks, anathema not only because it jeopardized the principle of class solidarity above all, but because, in their view, feminism in Russia prior to the 1917 Revolution was right-wing.[32] If the Zhenotdel provoked fears of female separatism, its existence would be justified in relationship to one of the most pervasive and divisive splits within the Soviet Union, that between urban and rural life. In 1923 Stalin wrote that the aim of the Zhenotdel was to encourage more active participation by rural women in the construction of Soviet life.[33]

Much of the controversy surrounding the Zhenotdel, as well as the conflicts and tensions concerning the implications of equality between the sexes, came to a head at the end of 1925, when the marriage laws were revised. It was proposed that unregistered marriages be recognized, thus permitting alimony even in unofficially sanctioned relationships. Public debates on the marriage laws were widespread, and they accentuated the sharp conflicts between urban and rural Russians on the woman question. This is not to say that urban dwellers, or even party members, for that matter, were enthusiastic supporters of female liberation. While it is true that the revision of the marriage laws was designed to protect women, it was precisely woman's legal status as "victim" that is symptomatic of the extreme ambivalence, within Soviet society, toward female equality. Only Kollontai insisted, as Beatrice Farnsworth puts it, "that the new marriage law be based, not on the demeaning assumption of a man's economic responsibility toward a woman, but on the socialist assumption of equality between the sexes and on society's collective responsibility toward its members in need."[34]

Farnsworth says of the marriage code controversy that "it crystallized the Communist Party's attachment to familiar images of women."[35] But what is striking to a contemporary feminist, looking at the first decade or so of socialist change in the Soviet Union, is not so much the "attachment to familiar images of women" of which Farnsworth speaks, but rather the fact that, despite Marxism's rather problematic relationship with the woman question, issues concerning women and sexual politics were so much a part of public debate and controversy. To be sure, much of the discussion was centered around women's traditional roles as wives and, in particular, as mothers. Nonetheless, the sheer extent of the discussion suggests that the familiar feminist slogan, "the personal is political," has immediate relevance for the history of socialist change in the Soviet Union.

Since my primary concern is with how the woman question was posed in the narrative and visual terms particular to the cinema, an examination of the theory and practice of montage is in order. In its narrowest definition, montage refers to film editing, but for Soviet filmmakers montage meant much more than the arrangement of individual pieces of film to form meaningful wholes. Montage became the quintessential technique of an art form devoted to dynamic movement and dialectical tension. Indeed, montage would demand nothing less than a new kind of film viewing, recalling the function of *priem ostranenie,* or the device of "making strange," the defamiliarization of habitual perception which the Russian formalists ascribed to literature.[36] Whether by fragmenting a scene into its constituent parts, or by creating unexpected juxtapositions of images, montage demanded active engagement of its viewers. Pudovkin described this process as one of the most distinct features of the cinema:

The cinema is in a sense a potential mirror, directly representing events in the wholeness of their dialectical complexity. In the wholeness of this reflection resides a profound force irresistibly dragging the spectator himself into participation in the creative process.[37]

Eisenstein wrote in similar terms of this new spectator "being drawn into the process as it occurs":

A work of art, understood dynamically, is just this process of arranging images in the feelings and minds of the spectator. It is this that constitutes the peculiarity of a truly vital work of art and distinguishes it from a lifeless one, in which the spectator receives the represented result of a given consummated process of creation, instead of being drawn into the process as it occurs.[38]

Whatever differences there were among Soviet filmmakers in defining montage, the active spectator is a central and common figure. Indeed, the most influential theories of montage from Soviet filmmaking of the 1920s share a preoccupation with the opposition of activity and passivity. In other words, cinema based on the principles of montage would eradicate any association between passivity and the cinema. Cinema was conceptualized as the embodiment of active, self-conscious awareness in distinct contrast to a cinema of what Vertov described as "magic" and "fragrant veils":

We oppose the collusion of the 'director-as-magician' and a bewitched public.
Only consciousness can fight the sway of magic in all its forms.
Only consciousness can form a man of firm opinion, firm conviction.
We need conscious men, not an unconscious mass submissive to any passing suggestion.
Long live the class consciousness of the healthy with eyes and ears to see and hear with!
Away with the fragrant veil of kisses, murders, doves, and sleight of hand!
Long live the class vision!
Long live the kino-eye![39]

There would be no place for the passive spectator in Soviet cinema. Passivity was the enemy, and it adopted a variety of other forms. In the most obvious sense, bourgeois cinema was targeted as epitomizing the rigid formulae of dramatic construction and the strictly conventional organization of space and time to which montage would offer striking alternatives, through principles of radical juxtaposition and the uniquely cinematic construction of space and time. In other contexts, filmmakers insisted on the special properties of the film medium in contrast with other literary forms, such as prose and theater. These forms do not necessarily breed passivity on their own terms, but they seem inert when compared with the properties of action and movement so central to the cinema. Pudovkin remarked on a playwright who, in the midst of writing about aviation, realized that the subject matter was more appropriate to the cinema. Pudovkin noted that the "full richness [of aviation] can be mastered and transmitted to the audience only by direct representation of events so far-reaching in scope and occurring in such dimensions that they cannot possibly be accommodated on the stage of a the-atre."[40] The duality of activity and passivity also would be evoked in a more subtle but nonetheless distinct way to insist upon the difference between literary methods and cinematic ones. Consider, for instance, Kuleshov's remarks on the filmic method:

In order to think in scenario terms about the "triumphant explosion of a dam" or the "charging of hostile forces into a city," what is needed is not a literary method but a filmic one—in shots: galloping horses, marching infantry, explosions, and so on, imagining them as if on screen visually.[41]

One senses that "method" here concerns not just the forms, but the subjects most appropriate to them, and that scenes of male aggression are, in Kuleshov's view, more appropriate to the dynamic activity of motion pictures than to literature.

Kuleshov's images not withstanding, there is little in the writings of Soviet filmmakers to suggest that montage is a particularly male endeavor, or that female subjects lend them-selves readily to montage treatment. True, one of Kuleshov's experiments in the practice of montage was the construction of a female figure from "the lips of one woman, the legs of another, the back of a third, and the eyes of a fourth. We spliced the pieces together in a predetermined relationship and created a totally new person, still retaining the complete

reality of the material."[42] Such an experiment may well demonstrate the powers of montage, but it demonstrates as well a
persistent male fantasy associated with the cinema, to create
an idealized, nonthreatening, female form.[43] However, Kuleshov's re-creation of a woman recalls Vertov's definition of the
kino-eye in terms not quite so gender-specific: "I am kino-eye.
From one person I take the hands, the strongest and most
dexterous; from another I take the legs, the swiftest and most
shapely; from a third, the most beautiful and expressive
head—and through montage I create a new, perfect man."[44]

But whether male or female, these cinematic creatures
evoked by Kuleshov and Vertov attest to montage as a means
of mastery, as power over the raw material of individual fragments of film. Through montage, cinema becomes a technology capable of transforming the human form. In his early
writings on film, Eisenstein is quite explicit about this function of montage. He distinguishes between the individual,
isolated shot, the "montage cell" or the "photo-fragment of
nature," and the combination of these shots in montage
sequences. "The shot's tendency toward complete factual
immutability is rooted in its nature," Eisenstein writes. "This
resistance has largely determined the richness and variety
of montage forms and styles—for montage becomes the
mightiest means for a really important creative remolding of
nature."[45]

The polarity of activity versus passivity, with the attendant
implications of mastery and creative remolding, lend themselves easily to the critique of binary opposition that has been
central to feminist examinations of culture and theory. Hélène
Cixous's observations on the subject are particularly relevant
here:

Organization by hierarchy makes all conceptual organization subject to man. Male privilege, shown in the opposition between

activity and passivity, which he uses to sustain himself. Traditionally, the question of sexual difference is treated by coupling it with the opposition: activity/passivity.[46]

The relative absence of concrete, flesh and blood women in the writings of Soviet filmmakers on montage should not obscure the pervasive and obsessive sense of duality that characterizes the theorizing of montage. Indeed, that duality is every bit as indicative of a system preoccupied, even if (or especially if!) subliminally, with differences of gender. Through the oppositions of activity and passivity, and technology and nature, montage is defined as an instrument of symbolic mastery—dialectic, perhaps, but dialectic only insofar as relationships between individual pieces of film, or between film and the spectator, are concerned. In terms of a relationship between the filmmaker and the film material, the boundaries between subject and object remain fixed and secure.

For all the claims of Soviet filmmakers that montage conquers passivity, however, the drama of the opposition between the poles of activity and passivity is reenacted, again and again, in films of the 1920s. In montage practice, these oppositions *do* acquire the definite shape of gender difference. Consider the film that contains what undoubtedly remains to this day the most famous example of the powers of montage: Eisenstein's 1925 film *Potemkin*. The famous Odessa-steps sequence is a brilliant demonstration of montage as a system of rhythm and contrasts, as the creation of a uniquely cinematic sense of space and time wherein referential space and time are virtually transformed, and as a complex network of visual and narrative signifiers. However, despite Eisenstein's claims that *Potemkin* was structured as an "organic whole" and as a five-part tragedy, the relationship between this famous sequence and other parts of the film, particularly the conclusion, is unclear, and less organic than Eisenstein claims.[47] The confusion stems, to a large extent, from the ambiguous function of female figures in the film and, in particular, from the relationship between those figures and the masses which the film ostensibly celebrates.

The narrative of *Potemkin* is defined, initially, by the opposition between officers and sailors aboard the battleship, with a slab of maggot-infested meat functioning as the symbol of this particular management's disregard for its workers. After a group of sailors have refused to eat soup containing the meat, officers order another group of sailors to shoot them. The second group eventually refuses, and the bonds of revolutionary and fraternal solidarity are forged. The sailors win the struggle to control the ship, but with one enormously symbolic fatality, the death of Vakulinchuk, the sailor who functioned as a political leader and organizer.

The struggle between sailors and officers is immediately recognizable, of course, as a class conflict. The two groups pitted against each other are relatively homogenous, for each opposing camp wears its own, identical uniform, and while there are some differences among the men belonging to each side, they are by and large interchangeable. The only brief visual contrast, in terms of the men's appearance, is provided by the ship's priest. Cloaked in a long robe and wearing long hair and a full beard, he is distinctly and remarkably different from the other men. This is a contrast which serves, however, to reinforce the oppressive solidarity of the church and the government, for despite his appearance, the priest is unquestionably an ally of the ship's officers.

When the ship docks at Odessa, Vakulinchuk's body is displayed for public view. Visitors swarm to the docks, paying their respects and bringing gifts to the sailors. Women appear here for the first time in the film. At the same time the crowds—which, during the battle on the ship, were relatively homogenous—become a varied mixture of old and young, rich and poor, politically militant and religiously pious. Thus, there is a movement away from the homogeneity of the groups involved in the class struggle on the ship, and toward the heterogeneity of the crowds at the port. At the same time, different kinds of details are isolated. Indeed, the attention of the film seems to shift decidedly away from the male form that dominates the film up to this point, and onto the female form.

The harmony between the sailors and the residents of the town is brutally interrupted by an attack on the well-wishers at the Odessa steps, announced by the infamous title that reads "Suddenly . . ." If the crowds portrayed at the port are a diverse mixture, the Odessa-steps sequence focuses more intensively, particularly through the selectivity of the close-up, on those bodies which are particularly vulnerable to the aggression of the soldiers. All of the female victims—and most of the close-ups are of women—appear to be mothers with children, and they attempt, in vain, to protect their charges from attack. In addition, the elderly and infirm are paid particular attention. During this sequence, the alternation between long shots and close-ups continues to be a central device, as it was during the struggle on board ship. But here, long shots of the people attempting to flee reveal frenzied movement and chaos, the close-ups are more exaggerated, and the faces more isolated. In other words, the Odessa-steps sequence takes the principles of contrast in montage structure to the extreme. The principle of homogeneity, characteristic of the representation of the men on the ship, here is applied to the extreme as well, for the soldiers are seen now as a set of legs marching in precision down the steps, then as a group of anonymous shadows cast over the victims. The concluding images of the sequence are of a baby carriage, abandoned when a young mother is killed, rolling down the steps; a young male student shrieking in terror; a wild-eyed cossack brandishing his sword; and an elderly woman in pince-nez, her eye put out, presumably by the cossack.[48] This is the only time that an attacking soldier is portrayed in close-up, and the juxtaposition of images of him and the elderly woman make for a striking encounter of brutality and victimization, while the young man observes helplessly.

The remainder of the film documents the growing political power of the revolutionaries. The battleship Potemkin is joined by other ships. During this section of *Potemkin,* shots of the individual men tend to focus on the bond between the sailors and the machinery of the ships. There is an abrupt shift in tone in this last section of the film, and it is signalled by another famous series of images. Through the creative manipulation of montage, three stone lions appear to be rising, thus functioning as an appropriate metaphor for the change in the Russian people, asleep, then awake, then ready for action. While montage legitimates such abrupt shifts, the changes that occur in the last section of the film—from the abstract symbolism of the stone lions to the idealized identification of the men with the machinery of the ships—speak also to a fundamental incoherence. Far from "exposing," "laying-bare," or "drawing one into the process as it occurs," montage in this case functions to naturalize the gap between the idealized abstraction of the last section of the film, and the concrete detail so central to the Odessa-steps sequence. It is as if the Odessa-steps sequence, with its frenzied movements and its predominance of female bodies, functions as *Potemkin*'s dark continent, from which the film emerges into the bright light of abstraction, homogeneity and revolutionary brotherhood—into, that is, a world populated once again exclusively by men.

Potemkin is marked by the impossible reconciliation of the abstract and the concrete, qualities that the film has defined as male and female, respectively. Indeed, the female body in *Potemkin* comes to represent the flesh in an absolute sense, that is, flesh as an excess, a superfluousness, which resists the pro-

cess of abstraction. As noted above, women do not appear in
Potemkin until the representation of crowds of people paying
their respects to the body of Vakulinchuk. The women first
seen have relatively simple functions, signified by their clothing and their body language: poor women in headscarves, expressing grief; bourgeoise women with parasols, expressing
curiosity. An interesting contrast is provided by several shots
of a woman who shakes her fist in anger. This marks the first
overtly political response to Vakulinchuk's death (and her
clenched fist aside, her response seems to be as emotional as it
is political). The political momentum quickens when the camera shifts to a young man, who reads a political tract to the
crowd. The crowd's growing anger is signified by the kind of
abstraction of which Eisenstein was so fond: several close-ups
of clenched (male) fists, none of which can be read as belonging to a single man in the crowd. Women in the crowd
respond in anger as well, but not with the same degree of
abstraction. While it is tempting to read the sequence as
establishing a clear opposition between male and female
modes of response to the death of Vakulinchuk, with men
responding "politically" and women responding "emotion-
ally," the differences articulated here are not quite that obvious. Indeed, the woman continues to speak, and to have an
effect on the crowd, so that it is difficult to know where the
emotional ends and the political begins. What sets apart the
representation of the woman is the way in which her body
connotes not only grief, anger, and outrage, but flesh, the
concrete, the very realm of the corporeal itself. Only from the
male body does the kind of abstraction emerge—in the form
of the series of clenched fists—that is central to Eisenstein's
conception of montage.

Given the rigid sexual polarity that defines the structure of
Potemkin, I find it extremely problematic to assume that the
excess associated with the female body can be described as an

instance of cinematic *écriture,* of a visual signifying practice
that subverts the duality of male and female, of activity and
passivity. Barthes refers to a still of the woman in question to
describe the "obtuse meaning," a signifier without a signified,
"the supplement that my intellection cannot succeed in ab-
sorbing, at once persistent and fleeting, smooth and elu-
sive . . ." Describing a profile of the woman raising her fist,
Barthes remarks on her hair, pulled back into a bun:

[I]t contradicts the tiny raised fist, atrophies it without the reduc-
tion having the slightest symbolic (intellectual) value; prolonged by
small curls, pulling the face in towards an ovine model, it gives the
woman something touching (in the way that a certain generous
foolishness can be) or sensitive—these antiquated words, mystified
words if ever there were, with little that is revolutionary or political
about them, must nevertheless be assumed. I believe that the obtuse
meaning carries a certain emotion.[49]

While Barthes's notion of the obtuse meaning suggests the
release of an emancipatory femininity, this third meaning is
not fixed within the boundaries of gender. Indeed, the quality
of obtuseness seems to transcend the boundary lines of gender. While this may well be an attractive feature of Barthes's
analysis, it is also problematic, for it is utopian in the sense
that it represses, rather than engages, the duality of gender.
The third meaning privileges the feminine without any consideration of how, within the narrative and visual economy of
the film, the terms "male" and "female" are rigidly opposed.
Put another way, men and women in *Potemkin* (and the film
does not go so far as to problematize the conflation of mas-
culinity with men, femininity with women) are differentiated
sharply in relation to Barthes's "obtuse meaning." And obtuse
meanings notwithstanding, in *Potemkin* men and women are
designated as occupying radically different positions. The
image of the woman whose hair overwhelms the raised fist

serves narrative and ideological ends that may not be on the same level of determinacy as other aspects of the film, but which are shaped by the tension between activity and passivity.

The status of *Potemkin* as a tribute to nascent revolutionary consciousness is complicated by the oppositions which inform the narrative and visual structure of the film. Any affirmation of the power of the masses is undermined considerably by the sexual dichotomy that informs the film. My point is not to critique sex-role stereotyping (men as agents, women as victims), to which one can always facilely respond that Eisenstein was only a creature of the dominant sexual stereotyping of his time. Rather, my point is that sexual opposition informs the tension between the concrete and the abstract, a tension which is central to the textual workings of the film. Yet another famous image of the film shows a pince-nez, with which the ship's physician had examined the maggot-infested meat, dangling from a pile of rope, after the physician has been thrown overboard (fig. 1.1). This image has received much attention as an example of the metaphoric possibilities of montage, drawing on Roman Jakobson's distinction between metaphor and metonymy as the two predominant figural axes.[50] Drawing on the example of the pince-nez, Christian Metz suggests that it is more to the point to analyze just how metaphor and metonymy intertwine in a given film, than to attempt to categorize them absolutely:

. . . the pince-nez conjures up in the spectator the representation of the doctor himself (that is why it is there): synecdoche. But in the preceding images we saw the doctor wearing the pince-nez: metonymy. The pince-nez connotes the aristocracy: metaphor. But it can do so only because the nobility—outside the diegesis, in the society of the time: another level of the 'referent'—liked to wear pince-nez: metonymy again. And so it goes on. It becomes clear that a filmic occurrence, in the particularity of its configuration, is more often

Fig. 1.1

distinguished by the exact form of the skein into which the metaphorical and metonymic strands are twisted, than by the presence
or absence of either element.[51]

The pince-nez has both metaphoric and metonymic functions,
and, as Metz suggests, it is more to the point to examine just
how those functions are intertwined. But the pince-nez raises
yet another question concerning cinematic figures. In the
scenes leading up to the conclusion of the Odessa-steps sequence, the pince-nez reappears, retaining its class connotations, but now defined primarily as a part of female attire.
Most strikingly, the woman whose eye is wounded, and who
is the last victim seen in close-up at the conclusion of the
sequence, wears pince-nez. The image of her horror-stricken
face, her right eye a gaping wound, makes for a striking contrast with the earlier image of the pince-nez belonging to the
ship's physician (fig. 1.2). However different they are meant
to be in other ways, the woman and the physician share a
certain blindness, underscored ironically by the pince-nez.

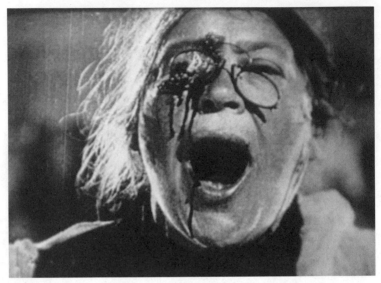

Fig. 1.2

The physician refuses to see the infected meat for what it is, thus contributing to the absolute division between the truths of the oppressed versus the lies of the oppressors. The woman's blindness is of another kind, for she naively and foolishly believes that the soldiers can be reasoned with, and leads a small delegation of women and elderly men up the steps. For men and women in *Potemkin,* cinematic figures operate in fundamentally different ways. Whether it is metaphoric or metonymic, the pince-nez belonging to the physician is a cinematic figure in the narrowest sense, a figure that removes one momentarily and abruptly from the diegesis of the film. It is an abstraction of the symbolic value of the doctor himself. In the case of the woman, however, the figure is not detached from the face, the eye, or the body. Rather, the woman's face marks a tension between the abstract and the concrete, between the metaphoric possibilities of film and the flesh which is made to resist such a departure from the immediacy of the events depicted in the film. There may be disagreement as to whether the physician's pince-nez is metaphoric or metonymic, but it is obvious that the pince-nez constitutes a cinematic abstraction. But what of the reappearance of the pince-nez on the woman's face? Is this also a rhetorical figure? To be sure, the close-up is an abstraction, but not an abstraction of the same order as the pince-nez seen in isolation during the mutiny. In *Potemkin,* the relationship of the figure of woman to the processes of abstraction is posed at the very least in an ambivalent way. Female figures connote the realm of the body to such an extent that, as in the present example, the pince-nez is identified with a woman's face, whereas previously in the film it stands alone to signify the physician.

Potemkin demonstrates, then, how in the practice of montage there is a persistent sexual dynamic at work. In Eisenstein's film, that dynamic takes the form of tension between the abstract and the concrete. In other films of the decade, the woman question raises different, yet related, issues of narrative and visual form. Kuleshov's 1925 film *By the Law,* for example, does not rely as extensively on the principles of montage as Eisenstein's films do. However, *By the Law* is a striking example of the ways in which strategies of cinematic adaptation also would be determined, even if somewhat more subtly than is the case with Eisensteinian montage, by sexual dynamics. *By the Law* suggests some fundamental ways in which Soviet narrative film would engage with other narrative forms, and how issues of gender are central to these narrative explorations. The film is an adaptation of Jack London's 1907 story "The Unexpected." The title of London's story refers to the forces which occur without logical or foreseen predictability. The characters in the story are a group of gold miners in the Yukon who respond in different ways to the "unexpected." Of the group, it is Edith, the only woman, who is best equipped to react when, without any apparent motivation, Michael Dennin—another member of the group—kills two men. Dennin is about to kill Edith and her husband Hans, but Edith stops him. Even in such a crisis, a sense of law emerges in Edith's response; she prevents her husband from killing Dennin out of revenge. She insists that they hold a trial, where Dennin is found guilty and then hanged.

Edith's respect for the law is presented in the story as a positive force. It is assumed that even when a "shuffling" of the "real and the unreal into perplexing confusion" occurs, there remains a fundamental sense of order, of a law to be obeyed, of a structure of civilization that cannot be violated.[52] It should not be surprising that Edith performs this function, for it is reminiscent of the traditional stereotype of woman as the upholder of morality. Yet at the very moment that Edith stresses the importance of the law, another perspective appears, a figure of otherness, suggesting that Edith's response needs to be situated within a historical context. This is the perspective of the Indians who refuse to meddle in "white man's trouble." They listen, however, to Dennin's confession prior to his death, and they witness the hanging. The short story closes with the Indians' perception of what has occurred: "But the Indians remained solemnly to watch the working of the white man's law that compelled a man to dance upon the air."[53] This conclusion represents a shift in perception, so that Edith's respect for the law is understood at once as necessity and absurdity. The short story juxtaposes the detailed working through of a response, perceived from within, with the vision of that response as an image, perceived from without. The juxtaposition relies on the figure of woman as both inside and outside white man's laws. Indeed, when read in feminist terms, the story historicizes the law in a curious way, for it is a woman who insists most forcefully upon the letter of the law, but it is only when the Indians appear at the conclusion of the story that the law is represented, in a critical light, as the law of white men.

The characters in Kuleshov's film bear the same names, and they are similarly located in a desolate, isolated space where they are driven to expose the most fundamental attributes of their race. Yet the historical and political dimensions of that process emerge in a fundamentally different way in *By the Law.* The gold miners form a miniature class society in which Dennin works the hardest while the others profit from his labor. Hence Dennin's crime is read, in the film, as evolving from a kind of proletarian rage, for he attempts to rid himself of his oppressors. Edith still respects the law, but the law is now a travesty, a symptom of bourgeois hypocrisy. Hence, in Kuleshov's reading of the London story, Edith's function as a woman is to be all the more identified with the law. Here, the law no more responds to a sense of genuine civility than does the picture of the English queen which hangs pretentiously on the wall during Dennin's trial. Nor is the law allowed to triumph in the film, for Dennin somehow survives the hanging and returns to the cabin with the noose still around his neck.

By the Law is more clearly demarcated in its political dimensions than London's story, particularly in terms of a class dynamic. Yet, if one aspect of the transposition of London's story to the screen is a more explicit rendering of political content, there is, simultaneously, an intensification of traditional narrative elements. More central to the film than to the short story is the space of the cabin, within which nearly all of the film takes place. Just as the characters exist as a miniature class society, so the space in which they move is both home and public world. Thus the rituals that occur in the cabin have a bizarre claustrophobic quality. The simple ritual of a meal shared by this makeshift family is transformed into bloody warfare by Dennin's rebellion. Rhyming with the domestic ritual of the meal is the makeshift trial and hanging, a public ritual which is again disturbed by Dennin's unexpected appearance at the cabin. Dennin's previous intrusion brought death. This intrusion, in equally unexpected fashion, brings life. *By the Law* plays, then, on the tensions resulting from the confusion of the realms of domestic and social life; of ordinary civilization and civilization transposed, as it were, to a desolate countryside.

A different kind of ritual occurs between the domestic ritual of the meal and the social ritual of the trial and execution. This is Edith's birthday party. The scene is introduced by shots designating the coming of spring. Through this change from the winter atmosphere that has dominated the film, a change in the relationship between the characters is announced. Dennin offers Edith a birthday present—his pocket watch. In preparation for the party, Hans gives Dennin a shave. Striking close-ups of the razor and Dennin's Adam's apple throbbing violently indicate the possibility that Hans finally might seek revenge on the murderer. That he does not indicates clearly a change in the relations between the two men. For the first time, Dennin is allowed to sit at the table with the couple, and he then explains why he killed the two miners. He wanted the gold—all the gold—for his mother. Dennin's confession occurs via flashbacks to a room where Dennin's mother sits at a table with a birthday cake on it. He enters bearing suitcases full of gold and says: "And you said that I was born to be hanged." Mother and son embrace as that scene dissolves to the present tense of the cabin, where the three characters sob as the candles on Edith's birthday cake burn away, destroying the cake.

The birthday party is a privileged moment in the film. It is the only occasion where there is a departure from the strictly present tense that not only dominates the film but also seems to suffocate the characters. The vision of Dennin's mother is in the past-tense and in an imaginary future at the same time. It is at this moment in the film that the present is joined to a past— the past of a real family, of a real parent-child relationship—in short, to a past of origins. At the same time, the ritual of the birthday party functions as a synthesis between the meal and the trial. Dennin finally sits down with his captors, ironically enough more as their equal than at any other moment in the film. He is portrayed as participating in their ritual rather than intruding upon it, and in speaking of his crime, he provides a kind of prelude to the trial. Perhaps most strikingly, the addition of this scene serves to displace Edith from the moral and narrative center that she occupies in the short story. For by endowing Dennin with a past and with a mother to whom he is devoted, the film shifts its center to him.

While there are several changes made in the transposition of the London story to the screen, the addition of the birthday party scene stands out precisely because it is so distinctly unlike the general tone of the short story. In fact, its source is radically different than the London story: according to co-scenarist Victor Shklovsky, it is based on a scene in Dostoevsky, added to the film to make it "more Russian."[54] The structure of the scene could indeed be seen as typically Dostoevskian. One is immediately reminded of *Crime and Punishment:* of Raskolnikov's attachment to his mother; of the pocket-watch, once his father's, that Raskolnikov takes to the old pawnbroker; and of his murder of the pawnbroker. One thinks also of a recurrent motif in Dostoevsky's novels: confessions at parties and social gatherings. Here, the scene which most immediately comes to mind is the birthday party in *The Idiot.* The event is in honor of Nastasya's birthday, and she proposes a game in which the guests must confess their most evil deed. One man committed a robbery for which another was accused; another wrongly accused an old woman of theft while she was dying; and another played a cruel prank on a friend in love, a prank which motivated a series of disasters in the young man's life. Against the background of this bizarre game is the developing relationship between Nastasya and Prince Myshkin, and the various sums of money which are being offered the woman for her affections.

There are no direct correspondences between the birthday party in *The Idiot,* the murder in *Crime and Punishment,* and the scene in *By the Law;* and one could not say that the filmed scene is directly drawn and adapted from a single Dostoevsky novel. Yet, there are associations between the different scenes: a pocket-watch symbolic of a past; a young man's attachment to his mother; murder; the corrupting influence of money; the presence of an old woman near death; the social event where personal secrets are divulged. It is as if certain Dostoevskian themes are drawn together briefly, reassembled as it were, to form a scene with resonances in the novelist's work. These resonances function as an unconscious network of narrative. It is toward Dostoevsky, and the narrative tradition of which he is a part, that the film turns to create its own structure of motivation, of the past, of family origins; in order to resituate a male figure at the center of the film by endowing him with an Oedipal past.

The birthday party is a formal bridge between the murder and the trial-execution, partially because of the ritualistic quality shared by the three scenes, and partially because of the formal symmetries established between them. The birthday party scene is also set off from these scenes, in that it is the only scene of the film which can be described as personal. The ritual itself is one of family and friends, more so than the meal; and the gestures exchanged—again, ironically—signify a warmth and communion, previously reserved almost exclusively for Dennin's relationship with his dog. Most important, Dennin's relationship with his mother is presented as an object for contemplation by the others. The birthday party is structured by memory: the nostalgia-ridden memory of mother and of family rituals. For a brief moment, distinctions between oppressor and oppressed, executioners and victims, dissolve in the memory of past and family. The scene gives resonance to the desolate landscape that occupies, in the film, a never-never land between private relations and social conventions. In *By the Law,* a public space is built around the gaps between the most fundamental elements of civilization: parents, children, men, women, subsistence, shelter, nature. The film reads, then, as a dystopia in which the paring-down of civilization to those raw materials matches the emergence of class consciousness—hypocrisy in Edith and Hans, outrage in Dennin. The appearance of Dennin's mother introduces a tension between two radically different conceptions of woman; the one, Edith, an embodiment of class allegiances; and the other, the mother, an idealized figure that transcends class boundaries. No such opposition exists among the male characters, who may well be on opposite sides, but opposite sides of a shared identity.

By the Law is a socialist parable in which this gender differential is symptomatic of the tension between private and public space, a tension which is a central narrative mechanism in the film. These are dimensions added to the London story, partially and symbolically through the Dostoevsky reference, and even more so through a revision of the very foundations of the narrative experience. It is interesting in this context to consider the significance of London's "signature" to the film. The year before the release of *By the Law,* London's 1906 work *Why I Am a Socialist* was translated and widely distributed in the Soviet Union.[55] London is perhaps the source of Kuleshov's film more as a pamphleteer than as a short-story author (not unlike Chernyshevsky as a source of Lenin's political writings). In any case, London is hardly the kind of author to be associated with the middle-class narrative tradition. The Dostoevsky reference, and the birthday party scene, frame London's story in much the same way that the personal evocation of a past frames the film. The example appropriately shows, as well, how the function of narrative as social analysis—the writings of London, the influence of Chernyshevsky on Lenin's political formation—is intertwined with other narrative elements, and that their fusion depends crucially on the attendant shifts in gender identity.

My point is that, in whatever ways the Soviet cinema functioned to create a public sphere of socialism, the figure of woman is not only a central narrative and visual element, but also a figure upon which the tensions and conflicts of Soviet film narrative are projected. In the case of *By the Law,* the public sphere of socialism created in the film reconstitutes history through the adaptation of a short story. The evocation of Dennin's past and the attendant shifts in narrative structure give the film much more of a traditional gender configuration. Since Kuleshov's film does not deal with the contemporary public sphere of the Soviet Union (at least not directly), it could be argued that this is not a particularly appropriate example of the efforts of Soviet filmmakers to engage directly with the contemporary issues of socialism. Nor is *By the Law* as informed by the principles of montage as other films of the period.[56] Consider, then, Eisenstein's *October,* a film commissioned to celebrate the tenth anniversary of the 1917 Revolution, which articulates many of the myths central to the socialist state's view of its own history and contains many well-known examples of montage.[57] The film was the subject of extended controversy, and critics differed sharply in their assessments.[58] *October* may well celebrate the working-class solidarity of revolution, but it does so in a way that draws heavily on a sexually polarized view of the world, not to mention the revolution. Whereas *Potemkin* demonstrates how sexual dichotomy informs montage structure, *October* illustrates a much more far-reaching duality. The film traces the course of events from the February Revolution of 1917, depicted as a mass uprising appropriated by the bourgeoisie, to the bloody clashes between Bolsheviks and members of the bourgeoisie that resulted, finally, in the success of the Bolshevik Revolution. The Bolshevik victory climaxes in the storming of the

Winter Palace, where the provisional government, with Kerensky in charge, is stationed.

October opens with the dismantling of a statue of Czar Alexander III, a powerful if somewhat obvious symbol of autocratic authority. The dismantling of the statue demonstrates not only the proletarian desire to topple the existing forces and to undo their rigid symbolism, but also the cinematic investment in such a process, for the sequence is a stunning demonstration of the powers of montage.[59] The implications of statues as symbols of repressive law and order are further developed in other sections of the film, including the famous "gods" sequence, in which the attributes of religion and patriotism are demonstrated to have common ideological and formal denominators.[60]

If the function of statues in *October* suggests the clash between the dead, immobile, and rigid orders of the reactionary past and the living, vigorous, and dynamic vitality of the Bolshevik present, it is a clash that is complicated by the sexual oppositions so central in the film. The battle between revolutionary and bourgeois forces is stunningly conveyed in a scene portraying an attack by the well-to-do, most of them women, on a young Bolshevik man during a demonstration. The attack occurs next to a bridge, and the subsequent raising of the bridge is ordered by the authorities to cut off the proletarian districts from the rest of the city. During the raising of the bridge, a young woman's body, her long hair draped over the separated bridge, becomes a sign of the victimization of the revolutionaries by bourgeois force. This sequence is characteristic of a curious sexual dynamic at work in the film. The attack on the young Bolshevik male is portrayed as a frenzied sadistic ritual. The women who attack the man bear the obvious marks of their privilege, but they are marks which also function to signify an excess, almost a parody of femininity. In an analysis of this scene, Pierre Sorlin notes that in

October, the class allegiance of men is not always obvious—that is, not always visible. However, women are immediately recognizable as either proletarian or bourgeoise. Clothing is one such indication of female class allegiance (simple and functional for proletarian women; exaggerated, frilly, and decorative in the case of bourgeoise women), and body language is another. For proletarian women, the body is "but an instrument," whereas bourgeoise women display exaggerated body movements and theatrical gestures.[61] If the women who attack the Bolshevik are excessively feminine, it is thus suggested that the Bolsheviks are, by contrast, either masculine or neuter. Yet, there is more to the representation of these women than the parody of femininity, for their attack on the young man is clearly meant to be understood as rape, emphasized by the umbrellas with which they beat him.[62] Hence, these women seem to represent a confusion of sexual identities.

The woman on the bridge represents another kind of femininity. As Sorlin notes, she is virtually the only woman in the film who does not have an immediately visible class allegiance; rather, she has characteristics that have been attributed, in the film, to both classes. If her flowing mane of hair is suggestive of sensual abandon, the viewer senses that such a signifier of femininity is only possible once her status as absolute object is assured. This status is assured by the fact that, not only is she dead, but she has appeared nowhere else in the film. Her sudden appearance on the bridge, immediately following images of a dead horse, thus may have less to do with the requirements of cinematic *écriture* than with the sexual polarity of the film.[63] If female agency leads to the kind of crazed sexual aggression seen earlier in the scene, then the most appropriate contrast is woman objectified in the most absolute way possible.

In *October,* the key event is the storming of the Winter Pal-

ace. The palace is surrounded by, and the provisional government thus protected by, an army of women. The women's
battalion is portrayed in such a way as to evoke the vicious
bourgeoise ladies in the earlier scene. The confusion of male
and female identities, suggested by the women's symbolic
rape of the Bolshevik and by their aggressive behavior, here
becomes quite literal. When two men approach the women
soldiers, they do not know whether to refer to them as male or
female, their confusion only abated by the recognition that
one of the women is from the same region, thus dispelling
momentarily sexual confusion in the name of common geo-
graphical roots. Similarly, the excess of femininity associated
with the bourgeoise women is, in the case of the women soldiers, exaggerated in parodic fashion. At one point the wom-
en soldiers are seen inside the Winter Palace in various states
of undress, applying makeup. They appear to be imitating the
gestures of femininity, and they do so with considerable awkwardness. If, as Sorlin suggests, bourgeoise women in *October*
are characterized by expansive body gestures, here there is a
preoccupation with the female body as flesh, in all shapes and
sizes, mostly abundant and large. And, if the class hatred so
apparent in the earlier attack by the women was transformed
into a rabid sexual revenge, here the sexual component is
taken a step further, for there is more than a hint of lesbian
identity among these women. Not surprisingly, the lesbianism
is presented just as mockingly as was the women's imitation of
femininity.

The representation of the women soldiers also entails a continuation of the statue motif. Already, in the sequence depicting the raising of the bridges, statues had acquired a somewhat more complex function than the appearance of the
statue of Alexander III, in the beginning of the film, would
suggest. After the bridges have been raised, two statues in the
city are depicted in relationship to the raised bridge: one of

the Sphinx, the other of Minerva. If other representations of statues in the film suggest much more unequivocally the opposition between two radically different orders—the frozen rigidity of the upper classes versus the vitality of the proletarians—here the opposition is not so rigid. The sphinx appears as something of a detached observer, thus mirroring the function that the bourgeoise women, who watch the spectacle of the raised bridge with great glee, acquire during the sequence. In this sense, of course, the sphinx does affirm the equation of the reactionary order with rigidity and immobility. But at the same time, the sphinx—half animal, half female—evokes the very process by which, in the scenes immediately preceding the statue's appearance, the victimization of the Bolsheviks was portrayed by the substitution of the young woman's dead body for the corpse of the horse. Similarly, the appearance of the statue of Minerva may well suggest, as does the statue of Alexander III, a reified established order, but it suggests as well an ideal of femininity which, the film has suggested thus far, is best achieved when women are corpses.

Two statues by Rodin, *Spring* (depicting a naked man and woman kissing passionately) and *The First Steps* (depicting a mother guiding the first steps of her child), serve as ironic commentaries on the women soldiers. Just before the initial surrender of the women's battalion, one woman soldier leans against the statue of the couple embracing, and appears to mourn her own loss of femininity, heterosexuality, or perhaps both. In the case of *The First Steps,* the irony comes from alternation; as a woman officer has her soldiers practice the techniques of assault, images of the statue are intercut, thus stressing the distance between the maternal ideal and this community of women.

Excess is, of course, no stranger to Eisenstein, but in *October* the extreme dichotomy that characterizes most of the female protagonists is striking.[64] Women are seen as either the car-

icatured femininity of the women with the umbrellas and the
women's battalion, or as the reified, frozen femininity of statues or corpses. Andrew Britton describes the portrayal of
women as a fundamental incoherence in the film, emerging
from Eisenstein's "undisguised revulsion" for women. Thus,
Britton describes the representation of the members of the
women's army in a scene where they are shown scantily
dressed, applying makeup and passing the time together:

. . . the women are, after all, the last people on earth one would ever
expect to see using a powder-compact. The imagery depends on the
sense that they are desecrating the palace; that they are monstrous
because they are like women, biologically (the vagina-armpit) and
ideologically (the powder-puffs); that they are monstrous because
they are *not* like women (their physique, their clothing, the hint of
Lesbianism); and that they are primarily monstrous because their
nakedness (the uncovering of the body for the only time in the film)
unleashes the return of the sexuality repressed in the male relationships.[65]

Britton's analysis of the film as a celebration of male brotherhood thus accentuates the interdependency of the repression of gay male sexuality, and the subsequent displacement,
onto female figures, of libidinal power which then becomes
threatening. The climax, as it were, occurs during the storming of the Winter Palace, which reverses, on a grander scale,
the symbolic rape of the Bolshevik that occurred earlier. For
the storming of the palace is the conquest, not only of the
women's battalion, but also of the aggressive pretensions of its
members. Several members of the women's battalion have
hidden in the Czarina's bedroom, which is a monument both
to statuary and to bourgeoise femininity. Revolutionaries pen-
etrate the room, and attack the objects in it with considerable
simultaneous glee and bewilderment. The women soldiers
cringe in fear. As Britton suggests, "[t]he women's courage is

either grotesque or insubstantial, and its total abeyance here to 'natural' timidity adds lustre to the potency of the Bolsheviks."[66] Indeed, the reaction of the women soldiers serves to deny the very possibility of female agency suggested during the raising of the bridges—a problematic possibility in any case, given its class dynamics.

It is perhaps tempting to argue that this troublesome representation of female agency has more to do with Eisenstein's particular disposition toward women than with the sexual politics of film narrative in the Soviet Union.[67] I would argue, rather, that Eisenstein's visions of the sexual contours of revolution offer a representation "in amazingly bold relief" (to borrow from Lenin's description of Tolstoy) of a dynamic that emerges in many Soviet films of the period. The unabashed sexism of the film notwithstanding, *October* opens a gap between the "feminine" and the "female," that is, between social and biological definitions of womanhood. Ironically, the roles most often ascribed to women's natural function, those of heterosexual partner and mother, only appear in the form of statues. That the center of the film, in terms of its representations of women, should be the women's battalion is significant in this respect. According to Cathy Porter, the Women's Shock Battalions and the Death Battalions, formed by the provisional government and supported by a right-wing feminist organization, were designed "to inspire the faint-hearted with their merciless resolve to fight the enemy to the death and to prove themselves the equals of men in battle."[68] Eisenstein might have found, of course, many examples of female militancy within the Bolshevik camp.[69] If the women's army becomes a peculiarly contradictory image in *October,* it may have to do with something other than Eisenstein's own psychic and emotional disposition. Porter says that the Bolsheviks protested the women's battalions, not out of any perceived inferiority of the women, but rather because the women were being used and exploited to prolong World War I.[70] On the other hand, Louise Bryant's account of the October Revolution suggests, at the very least, a patronizing attitude on the part of the Bolsheviks:

When the Soviet formally took over the government the women soldiers were given two months leave. The majority were ordered home and told to put on female attire because they were considered enemies of the revolution. There was a good deal of misunderstanding on both sides.[71]

One wonders, however, what the command to "put on female attire" signifies; whether the women were being punished, or restored to their proper place—at home and in dresses. Bryant herself is critical of the women's battalion, and stresses that women have fought and always will fight in Russia, but alongside of men, rather than in a separate sphere. One senses, therefore, that much of the negative fascination with the women's battalion (both in Eisenstein's film and in Russian culture at large) stems from the possibility of female autonomy. In *October*, female autonomy is portrayed as perverse and unnatural. Yet, at the same time, virtually *all* versions of female identity with any kind of active component are portrayed as perverse and unnatural. In other words, it is not clear where the line is drawn between perversity and normality as far as women are concerned. Hence the film stumbles in its own articulation of natural versus unnatural definitions of womanhood.

A final example will serve to illustrate how, in a film radically different from Eisenstein's though perhaps as extreme in its own way, woman functions as a problematic link between nature and culture. Alexander Dovzhenko's 1930 film, *Earth*, is an exploration of the possible integrations between the worlds of technology and nature. On the side of technology stand collectivized farming and socialist principles; on the side of nature, the cycles to which the lives of the peasants depicted in *Earth* are bound. In a different way than Eisenstein's *October,* Dovzhenko's film was controversial. It was made at the time of fierce battles over agricultural policy, when the "encouragement" of cooperative farming that had been the rule under NEP was replaced with forced collectivization by Stalin. *Earth* takes place in Dovzhenko's native Ukraine, where there was particularly strong resistance to collectivization.[72]

Dovzhenko is well known for his lyrical style, and the plot of *Earth* is quite simple, thus drawing attention more to the overall feel of the film than to the story itself. The film centers on a father and son relationship. At the beginning of *Earth,* an elderly man, Simon, dies in an orchard, surrounded by family and friends. His death is presented as part of the natural order of things, part of a cycle of death and rebirth. Indeed, the lives of the peasants in *Earth* seem to be totally integrated with the rhythms of the land and the seasons. The central conflict in the film stems from the relationship between Simon's son Opanas, who opposes collectivization, and Opanas's son Vasyl, who is an enthusiastic supporter. Vasyl leads the group which brings the first tractor to the collective, and the results are, as expected, quite positive. After a bountiful harvest, as Vasyl dances to celebrate, an angry kulak kills him in despair. In response to his son's death, Opanas requests that the funeral service be performed by the members of the collective rather than by the church. Throughout the film, religion has been presented as an obstacle to the success of collective farming. Opanas's request thus carries enormous symbolic weight. Indeed, Vasyl's untimely death—unlike his grandfather's death, Vasyl's is decidedly unnatural—is transformed into a positive force, for Opanas assumes his son's enthusiasm for collectivization. The sense of a nature-bound existence is reinforced at the conclusion of the film when Vasyl's mother gives

birth to another child, and Vasyl's female companion, distraught and despondent during his funeral, finds a new beau.
Indeed, the film is an affirmation of the relationships between
parent and child and between male and female lover as the
most basic ties between the social and the natural order.

The ideological and aesthetic aims of *Earth* are to accentuate and to celebrate the bond between human beings and the
cycles of nature, and more precisely, to define socialism as the
most appropriate link between them. What is not always clear
in the film, however, is the extent to which men and women
share equally in that bond. Consider, for example, the representation of the body in *Earth*. In ways reminiscent of *Potemkin,* women are represented much more as creatures of emotion and of the flesh than are men. It is women, for instance,
who demonstrate the excessive attachment to religion in the
film. True, the viewer is led to believe that, for the father, the
decision to reject a church service for his son is a serious and
difficult one indeed. However, the visual representation of
that attachment to the church is virtually exclusively female.
Another kind of excess characterizes the way in which women
are represented during the harvest. Men are portrayed as fully
a part of the work which they perform. Women's bodies, however, are put on display. When the women bend over to collect
the grain, their bare legs are exposed by their movements and
by the wind. Unlike other images of the harvest, here the camera lingers over the display of the female body.

There is a marked difference between the ways in which
male and female bodies function within the narrative and
visual framework of *Earth*. When Vasyl is killed, he is performing a joyful dance, celebrating the success of the harvest.
When his murderer mimics the dance at the conclusion of the
film, a clear opposition is established between the two men
and the two orders which they represent. The one, embodied
by Vasyl, is characterized by a body whose spontaneous move-

ments suggest the harmony and integration between human beings and the natural world. The other, embodied by Khoma, is characterized by an absolute inability for spontaneity, since his dance can only parody the ideal connection between Vasyl and nature, but not provide any meaningful substitute.[73] While this opposition between two men and two social orders seems quite clear-cut, the intervention of a distinctly female body complicates somewhat the neatness of the opposition. During the funeral of Vasyl, the grief of Natalka (his female companion) is represented by the thrashing movements of her naked body within a cottage, isolated from the family and friends. The function of the female body here reflects the way in which women in *Earth* have been defined. Natalka's expression of grief recalls the two ways in which the female body has been represented in the film—as an excess, here of grief, elsewhere in the film of religious sentiment; and as an object of display, emphasized here not only by the naked body, but also by its isolation. *Earth* appears, then, to affirm a profound difference in the ways in which human beings are identified with the cycles of nature, not only in terms of class but in terms of gender as well. In and of itself, this is hardly a particularly shocking or noteworthy observation. But there is more than sexual polarity per se at work. What is particularly interesting in *Earth* is the way in which the registers of class and sexuality collide. Even though *Earth* is most visibly concerned with the difference between socialism and its enemies, the narrative and visual differences that separate men and women in the film problematize the class oppositions rather than reinforce them.

The naked female body has a somewhat confusing function in a film so preoccupied with clear and simple oppositions between natural and unnatural forms. If she appears to embody life-giving force (a female function which provides a resolution to the film, when Vasyl's mother gives birth to another child) in contrast to the funeral, her movements are

also evocative of Vasyl's dance. One could read this connection between the expression of joy and the expression of grief
as a sign of the profound bond and connection between Vasyl
and Natalka. But Natalka's movements also function as the
visual and narrative passage from Vasyl's dance of life and joy
to Khoma's dance of death and desperation. The body of the
woman becomes, then, a figure upon which are projected the
similarities between representatives of the two orders, similarities which are otherwise unspoken in the film, that is,
unspoken in terms of the film's overt ideological and narrative
allegiances. Hence, the connection between nature and culture, between the patterns of agricultural life and those of
socialist collectivity, is made across the body of the woman, a
body defined as a pure element of nature.

For Eisenstein, the body of the naked woman in *Earth* was a
particularly striking example of how not to make a movie—or
more precisely, of how not to create an effective visual metaphor. In his 1944 essay, "Dickens, Griffith and the Film
Today," Eisenstein discusses Dovzhenko's film within the
context of issues raised by Griffith's film *Intolerance*. Eisenstein
takes Griffith's film to task for its inadequate and unsuc-
cessful motif of Lillian Gish rocking a cradle, a motif that
appears at intervals to unite the separate tales that comprise
the film. According to Eisenstein, Griffith

had been inspired to translate these lines of Walt Whitman, " . . . endlessly rocks the cradle, Uniter of Here and Hereafter," not in the
structure, nor in the harmonic recurrence of montage expressive-
ness, but in an isolated picture, with the result that the cradle could
not possibly be abstracted into an image of eternally reborn epochs
and remained inevitably simply a life-like cradle, calling forth deri-
sion, surprise or vexation in the spectator.[74]

Eisenstein's objection to the image of Gish rocking a cradle is
a critique of Griffith's handling of cinematic metaphor. Eisen-

stein's description of the cradle image as too "life-like" suggests that in order for the image to work, it needs to be more fully and convincingly abstracted—less like the other images in the film, for instance, less identifiable as a real cradle.

Eisenstein then claims that the naked woman in Dovzhenko's *Earth* constitutes a "nearly analogous blunder" to the image of Gish rocking the cradle. The woman is insufficiently abstract, says Eisenstein, particularly since her body is presented in long shot, rather than in close-up. As we have seen in *Potemkin,* the tension between the abstract and the concrete, a tension that frequently takes the form of the difference between medium or long shots and close-ups, is informed by a sexual dynamic. Eisenstein's own solution in *Potemkin* to the problem he raises in discussing *Earth* was to isolate close-ups of victims, most of them female, on the Odessa steps. These close-ups do not seem particularly abstract, especially when compared with the remainder of the film. However, they do separate the female body from the extraneous details that, according to Eisenstein, overwhelm and overpower the female body in *Earth.* According to Eisenstein, Dovzhenko sought, with the image of the woman's body, to create "an image of a life-affirming beginning," to contrast with the funeral procession. The spectator, says Eisenstein, "could not possibly separate out of this concrete, lifelike woman that generalized sensation of blazing fertility, of sensual life-affirmation, which the director wished to convey to all nature, as a pantheistic contrast to the theme of death and the funeral!" Eisenstein does not argue that the woman's body constitutes an inappropriate image, but rather that the way in which the image is constructed, with the objects of everyday life surrounding the woman's body, prevents the image from working successfully. In his words, "representational naturalism" interferes with "the embodiment of the conveyed metaphorical task."[75]

Aside from the obvious fact that both images portray

women, there is, in fact, little resemblance between the functions of the images in *Intolerance* and *Earth*. I do not think that
the woman's body in *Earth* is as obviously designated with a
precise metaphorical function as Eisenstein does; but more to
the point, what Eisenstein describes here as a problem of metaphor is more appropriately described as a problem of the
female body. However different their cinematic approaches to
the representation of the female body (long shots in the case of
Dovzhenko, close-ups in the case of Eisenstein), neither Eisenstein nor Dovzhenko is successful in creating the desired
abstraction. The problem posed here has less to do with the
composition of the individual shot, as Eisenstein would suggest, and more to do with the function of the female body in
relationship to the narrative and visual system of the film as a
whole. Despite the very different cinematic styles that these
two directors employ, the confusion that Eisenstein attributes
to Dovzhenko characterizes Eisenstein's own approach to the
representation of the female form. The point, of course, is not
who is more confused, but that the representation of the
female body should be posed as a problem of adequate
"abstraction."

That the female body does indeed suggest a problem of
representation is evident in the films discussed in this chapter.
In all four of them, woman has a disruptive function. In visual
and narrative terms, the figure of woman complicates some of
the principal oppositions upon which these, as well as other
films of the period, are based—between activity and passivity, between bourgeoisie and proletariat, and between
nature and culture. To be sure, these are oppositions of quite
different kinds. I have described the opposition of activity and
passivity as a key methodological issue in the concept of montage, which appears, in montage practice, in the guise of sexual dichotomy. Class conflict is the master code of Soviet film
of the 1920s, a thematic and narrative opposition that deter-

mines virtually all aspects of cinematic form. The relationship between nature and culture functions as a thematic support for class conflict, and those filmmakers in whose work nature has a significant role—Dovzhenko certainly, but also Eisenstein and Pudovkin—tend to be concerned with socialism as the expression of some kind of biological destiny. Yet, in the oppositions of class conflict and of nature and culture, women function in similar ways, whether it be to disrupt the category of class as a neat and clear-cut opposition of social and economic privilege, or to problematize the easy fit between nature and culture. The woman question in Soviet cinema of the 1920s is crucial and complex, engaging the methodological core of Soviet film style—the use of montage in *Potemkin;* the narrative strategies whereby Soviet filmmakers created an art form devoted to ideological change—the process of adaptation in *By the Law;* and the thematic oppositions that inspire narrative crisis and resolution—the tensions between the natural and the social worlds in *October* and *Earth.* I turn now to a more detailed examination of the narrative structures of individual films, each of which turns centrally on the woman question.

2. *Strike* and Displaced Vision

STRIKE (1925), Eisenstein's first feature film, demonstrates some of the same preoccupations as those I have described in *Potemkin* and *October.* I find *Strike* worthy of more detailed analysis, in part because it anticipates some of the questions concerning montage and sexual dichotomy, and class and gender, that are found in later films of Eisenstein and his contemporaries. As in *Potemkin,* there is a clear demarcation of men's and women's spheres, but in *Strike* it is less the female body per se which is scrutinized, than the space occupied by the female body—the space, that is, of domesticity and personal relations. Femininity emerges in *Strike,* as in *October,* as a contradictory entity, but *Strike* is less taken up with the rigid and extremely class-bound sexual stereotyping evidenced by the women's batallion or the murderous bourgeoise ladies with their parasols. In fact, of all of the films to be discussed in subsequent chapters, *Strike* would, I suspect, appear to be the least relevant to a discussion of Soviet cinema and the woman question. The context in which women appear in the film—the spheres of domestic and sexual relations—are quite emphatically marginal to the explicit and obvious concerns of the film as indicated by its title. However, it is precisely this apparent *lack* of engagement with the woman question that makes *Strike* a particularly interesting object of study. *Strike* demonstrates how a film that seems to be only

65

tangentially concerned with gender nonetheless explores, in profound and complex ways (profound and complex precisely because they are less immediately obvious), cinematic and political implications of gender and sexual identity. What I hope to demonstrate, then, is that the woman question is not at all the secondary issue that it appears to be in *Strike*.

Strike is on one level a relatively straightforward narrative which taps the growing tradition of socialist mythology. The film tells a story of the absolute and irreparable difference between capitalists and proletarians. Eisenstein draws on many different sources and incidents of the prerevolutionary past to depict the brutal repression of the workers' movement by the forces of capitalist reaction. A factory boss has tried unsuccessfully to put an end to clandestine revolutionary activity among his factory workers. After his own emissaries fail him, he arranges for the hire of professional spies. When a worker is accused of theft and hangs himself in desperation, the workers—partially as a result of preplanned activity and partially in spontaneous reaction to the worker's death—go on strike. The bosses use a variety of means to break the strike. One worker is captured and coerced into identifying some of his comrades; police disrupt strike meetings; and a group of underworld (literally: they live in barrels dug into the ground) subproletarians are hired as infiltrators to turn a peaceful march into a violent riot. The latter tactic is not wholly successful, but gives mounted police the excuse necessary to annihilate the workers and their families. The climax to the massacre is marked by one of Eisenstein's most famous demonstrations of montage, whereby an analogy is created between the killing of workers and the slaughter of animals. Finally, the film concludes with a word of advice to proletarians to "remember." The basic plot structure—this straightforward narrative of capitalist versus proletarian—at first glance seems to be rather standard socialist-realist fare.

The only missing element is a triumphant ending, and even that is provided in part. For while the workers are being slaughtered, the continued survival of the workers' movement is suggested by the one worker who refuses to sell out completely to the police.

Strike assumes knowledge of this basic story; it is the central story of revolutionary Soviet culture and the basic political lesson of socialism: the collective, positive strength of workers versus the corrupt and decadent power of the bosses. Yet, against that familiar background, many elements are complicated in such a way that the film acquires a narrative complexity obscured initially by the apparently simple opposition of boss and worker. Immediate attention is focused, for instance, not on the workers, and not on the boss—even though he is the first person seen in the film—but rather, on the boss's intermediaries, a factory foreman and an office worker who attempt to spy on the workers; and later, attention is focused on the actual spies hired for that purpose. Similarly, the early scenes of the film focus our attention, not so much on preparations for the strike, as on the intrusion of these spies into the workers' secret meetings. Once the strike has been declared, it is represented in a highly disjointed fashion. The suicide of the worker Jacob is followed by a frenzied pace of activity, and this provides one of the few instances of an overall view of strike activity. Immediately after the strike is declared, however, it is presented in a much more fragmented way. There are strike meetings, and the effect of the strike on both workers and bosses is apparent; but no overall image of strike strategy is created.

What becomes more important than the event of the strike itself are the relations of power underlying the strike. Sometimes these relations further demonstrate the absolute difference between capitalists and proletarians; at other times these relations are not easily assimilable or reducible to the class opposition central to the film. In the first instance, scenes of meetings of striking workers immediately followed by meetings of management clearly serve to expand upon the ideological and visual differences between the opposing camps. The workers' meetings are shaped by a combination of passion and democratic process, while the meetings of management are governed by stilted, excessive rationality, and a repression of the movement and fervor defining the masses. In the second instance, scenes from the workers' homes, followed by scenes of the bosses during their leisure time, continue to emphasize these differences, but they also suggest some parallel discord as well. The scenes of home life accentuate the isolation of the workers' movement, an isolation emphasized in the representation of the bosses' leisure time as well. Hence the class opposition of *Strike* collides with other oppositions. Quite frequently the collision is a function of sexual polarity.

In keeping with the principles of montage so central to Soviet filmmakers, contrast is fundamental. Rather than creating a vision of the workers' movement as an organic whole, *Strike* takes montage as an overarching principle of development, and focuses on particular elements of, and vantage points on, strike activity. Several years after *Strike,* Eisenstein would describe montage as dictated by the metaphor of collision (in opposition to what he understood as "linkage" in Pudovkin's montage practice). "By what then is montage characterized, and, consequently, its cell—the shot? By collision. By the conflict of two pieces in opposition to each other. By conflict. By collision."[1] Eisenstein's description is appropriate to the most stunning uses of montage in *Strike,* for the film is characterized overall by that sense of "collision" and "conflict."

Strike recalls, too, the ideal of *priem ostranenie,* or the device of "making strange" central to the writings of the Russian Formalists. *Strike* may be understood as "defamiliarization" in the sense that the disruption of a straightforward narrative prevents the political structure of the film from being understood as mere cliché and stereotype. There is no question that in this Eisenstein film, characters are drawn in absolute terms of good and evil. The workers are for the most part young and sturdy, and the bosses are elderly fat men who do little else than eat or sit at desks. This distinction becomes somewhat more problematic when the female characters in the film are taken into consideration. However, the division of male characters into the two opposing camps of good and evil is problematized as well, so that the very basis of stereotyped behavior and action is put into question.

The first five shots are extremely interesting in this respect. The film opens with a shot of factory smokestacks, followed by a close-up of a fat, greedy-looking Dickensian boss rubbing his chin. This close-up dissolves to a shot of office building corridors where workers are running to and fro, and another dissolve returns to the close-up of the boss, who leans back his head and laughs. While this man is presented with a minimum of context, his face and manner leave no doubt that he is a stereotypical capitalist. After this close-up, a forward tracking shot reveals the inside of the factory. Thus the opening of *Strike* reveals three views of the factory—its exterior, its administration, and its machines. These images are joined to the close-up of the boss, the only person in these images who is individualized through the selectivity of a close-up. And so, the opening of the film seems to declare, this is his factory. The boss seems to be watching the workers, although there is no visible spatial unity in the shots. The three views of the factory are disconnected and could well be three different factories. The close-up of the boss is unanchored and undefined within a context; behind him there is only an indistinct grey background. This discontinuity could be seen as representative of the boss's mastery of space and time—he is, after all, symbolic of the power that controls any factory, seen from whatever angle. Yet, this discontinuity also could be read as an indication of a weakness, that is, the fragmented nature of the boss's power. Ownership is undermined by fragmentation, and controlling vision is undermined by discontinuity. Right from the outset, then, Eisenstein suggests that the principles of film editing might serve to illustrate a dialectical thesis.

The straightforward, familiar story of *Strike*—the exposition of the contradiction between boss and workers, the eruption of the strike and its subsequent destruction by the superior brute force of the capitalists—is defamiliarized. *Strike* does not refer specifically to a single historical event, but rather condenses within the framework of a single strike many registers of political significance. *Strike* attempts to create a useable past, and the film reflects and acts upon the growing mythology of socialist culture. Yet, alongside the familiar in *Strike,* there is another organization of actions, another series of events. These form the underside of the strike, representing different angles and perspectives on the film's exposition of the social relations of capitalism.

The central relationship within that exposition, and within the straightforward narrative, is the power relationship between boss and worker. Still, even the relationship between boss and worker is not visualized directly. It is shown obliquely through the intermediary power of the factory foreman and, later, the spies. These intermediaries have neither the real (but potentially tenuous) power of the boss; nor do they have the potential (but unrealized) power of the workers. Their power consists of little more than the power to watch, to observe. In political terms, these intermediaries are powerful only insofar as they carry out and administer the orders of others. In cinematic terms, however, the power to observe—to determine image flow, to guide and direct the perception of the viewer— is of central importance. It is well known that Soviet filmmakers, and Eisenstein and Vertov in particular, claimed for cinematic representation a particular form of political urgency. What *Strike* demonstrates is a politics of cinematic form located, not in the subservience of film to a political signified, but rather in the articulation of a tension between the registers of political and cinematic significance.

There is a tension, then, between the (cinematic) power of the look and the (political) power of action, and it is from that tension that the narrative structure of *Strike* develops. Central throughout the film are the ways in which social relationships entail different ways of seeing. Put another way, *Strike* is concerned with spectatorship, with the ways in which events are viewed, and with the relationship between those ways of seeing, as they are depicted within the film and as they shape how *Strike* is perceived. Spectatorship develops in *Strike* as the representation of the power to see. When the boss arranges for the hire of spies, each of the four is presented in much the same way as was the boss at the beginning of the film: a close-up of each spy is followed by a dissolve, not to what each possesses (as was the case with the boss), but to an image of the animal whose name he bears (figs. 2.1 and 2.2). When the spies begin to gather information about the workers' meetings, the power of the workers is also represented in terms of vision, because their power is, initially, the power to obstruct vision. During the first part of the film, the foreman, as well as the spies, are prevented by the workers from eavesdropping. In fact, the spies are only twice successful in their work, both moments occurring near the end of the film. One spy manages to arrange for the arrest of a worker by photographing him as he removes a management notice from a display case; another spy engages the subproles to infiltrate the workers' march.

The first completed action in the film revolves around the activities of the workers. In spite of the spies, the workers continue to meet, and they print and distribute leaflets. The

Fig. 2.1

Fig. 2.2

power to obstruct vision is accompanied by another form of power, then, the power to carry an action through to completion—again, a form of power with specific narrative weight. The principle of initiation and completion of an action—completed in spite of the presence of the intermediaries, or uncompleted because of their presence—structures the narrative development of the entire film. A micrometer is stolen (initiating action); the worker Jacob is harassed by the intermediaries—the foreman and the office worker—and Jacob kills himself (completion). This indication of the power of management is immediately followed by the declaration of the strike, leading to a strike rally, while the two intermediaries in question watch furtively and helplessly. Throughout the film, the balance of power between capitalist and worker is determined, not so much by the actual outcome of each individual action, but by the relative strength of an intermediary in determining what that outcome will be. All actions in *Strike* are, in short, mediated, so that events are never simple processes involving just a beginning and an end, but rather always are determined by a complex network of agents and outcomes. Indeed, this Eisenstein film demonstrates a fascination with "middles," as opposed to beginnings and conclusions.

Because the range of actions is so complex in *Strike*, it is useful for narrative analysis to break the film down into principal segments. On the basis of the principle of action initiation and completion, the film can be divided into five major parts. The first two are dominated by the power of the workers, and the last two, by the downfall of the workers' movement. The third part of the film marks the pivotal shift in power. Each of the five parts has three components: an initiating action, the intrusion of an intermediary, and a result. In the first part, the initiating action is the workers' secret meeting, which is spied upon by the foreman, the office worker, and the spies hired by the boss. The result of the meeting is the

production of leaflets. In part two, the theft of the micrometer
functions as the initiating action. The factory foreman and an
office worker once again serve as intermediaries, harassing
the worker they suspect of the theft. This section concludes
with the worker's suicide. Parts three and four are characterized by more complex events. In part three, where there is a
decisive shift of power in favor of the bosses, two interrelated
series of actions occur. The first initiating action is the presence of workers at home. The intermediary here functions in a
more abstract sense than in the previous two parts of the film;
it is the boss himself, seen alone in a restaurant, who occupies
the same position, structurally, as did the spies, the foreman,
and the office worker in the previous sections. A shareholders'
meeting dramatizes the bosses' power to extend beyond their
immediate spatial or temporal frame of reference, as was suggested by the opening shots of the film. When the film returns
to scenes of the workers' home lives, there is discord and tension. The result initiates another chain of events as well: a
workers' meeting in the woods is disrupted by police, who are
yet another mediating force for the bosses. The use of force
causes the strikers to disperse. In part four, the two forms of
intermediary power—the spies on the one hand, the police on
the other—are consolidated. Here, the initiating action is provided by a worker who removes from display a poster put up
by management. A spy with a camera photographs the
worker, leading to his arrest. The arrest of the worker functions as an initiating action as well because another kind of
intermediary is introduced during his interrogation: a pair of
midgets, one male and one female, who dance on a table in the
background. The final result of part four is the worker's confession. In the final, fifth section of the film, the workers'
march provides the initiating action. Another kind of intermediary power, that of the subproletarians hired to infiltrate
the march, is introduced. Once their presence has produced

the desired effect (a riot), the police again intervene. The conclusion to part five is the slaughter of the workers by the police.

This division of the film into five parts makes clear the structural link between the spies, the police, and the extreme caricatures (the subproles and the midgets) that populate the film, for each dramatizes the power of the rich over the poor, and stands as a substitute for the bosses. Hence, a principle of displaced vision is central to the film; the battle between workers and capitalists is engaged through a series of substitutes as far as the capitalists are concerned. Also, the division of the film into these five major sections reveals the importance of the principle of displaced vision as not just a central theme, but as the basis for the organization of opposing terms. Thus, if the balance of power seems to be tipped toward the workers at the end of the second part of the film, it is only in part because the strike has been declared. It is also because the workers succeed in humiliating the intermediaries—the foreman and the office worker—by forcing them to ride in wheelbarrows to the riverbank, where they are thrown into the water.

The demise of the workers' power begins in the third part of the film. This section is particularly interesting for a number of reasons. For the first time, boss and worker are seen in direct opposition to each other via the alternating montage of the sequence; there are no spies. The opposition occurs in cinematic space and time, and not in real space and time—that is, the opposition articulated here relies on the figural properties and the ideological charge of the tension between boss and worker, rather than on the literal obstruction of the workers' activities by the boss's emissaries. Another kind of displaced vision occurs, in a sense replacing the spies; the workers and bosses alike are seen, not in the context of the factory, but in the context of leisure time and home life.

Fig.   2.3

To be sure, the spies represent a perspective, and home life represents a space, an activity; these are not commensurate terms. However, they are commensurate in the sense that the spies represent a decentered position which is then taken up by the narrative and visual structure of the film itself—specifically, through alternating montage—as what lies beyond the immediate boundaries of strike activity becomes apparent. The sequence begins and ends with the domestic lives of the workers. Because of the strike, a worker has time in the morning to spend with his child, and a couple joyfully bathe their child together. A dinner where a collective spirit prevails is opposed to images of the factory owner eating alone at a restaurant (figs. 2.3 and 2.4). Alternating montage is thus used to explore the margins of factory activity per se.

Various substitutions in the alternating tracks between workers and owner occur. The meeting of the workers in the woods proceeds in linear fashion, alternating with images of

Fig.   2.4

the boss alone in his factory office, and police polishing their boots. The stunning climax of this section is the shareholders' meeting at which four grotesquely fat capitalists quickly ignore the strikers' demands and move on to more urgent business: the demonstration of an ornate juicer which one of the men has acquired. The shareholders' meeting alternates with the continuation of striking workers meeting in the woods, and the demonstration of the juicer coincides with an attack by mounted police. Finally, the focus shifts back to the domestic scene which began the sequence. But now, discord reigns. A wife blames her husband for the lack of food, and a husband takes possessions to sell against his wife's will. The home, initially presented as an alternative space to that of the factory, is invaded by the same power relations operative at the workplace. The resolution of an action is achieved, in this section of the film, through the boss, presented here as more of an abstract entity than as a particular individual. Thus, the relationships of power have shifted. As long as the owner has access to power, there is no refuge from the factory, no way to escape the penetration of capitalist values into the home. Nor does the capitalist ever cease to be a factory owner. When the bosses are ostensibly enjoying their leisure time, their fascination with the juicer coincides with the attack by mounted police. The demonstration of the juicer is so precisely intertwined with the police attack that it functions almost as an orchestration, as a kind of machinery setting the attack into motion. Alternating montage functions, then, as a form of displacement in the sequence, establishing a series of relations with constantly shifting terms, with constant substitutions: home for factory, police for boss, juicer for weapon.

It is significant that the shifting of the balance of power in favor of the boss should occur at precisely the point that domestic space is represented for the first time on the screen. The differing perspectives of private and public life form another oblique angle through which the central power relationship of boss/worker is perceived. With the introduction of private, domestic space in this central section of the film, we see another kind of intermediary figure: woman. Women in *Strike* are not defined immediately as either capitalists or workers; nor are they emissaries in the same way as the bosses' allies. Like the intermediaries, however, women always appear in an oblique context in the film. Women are seen almost uniquely in the context of the male-female couple. During the strikers' meeting in the woods, women are actively and visibly present, but this occurs only after women have been introduced within the context of domesticity. It is as if women can only be represented as active participants in the strike once they have been assigned their proper roles—at home. Women's roles within the male-female couple suggest in turn two different registers: on the one hand, domestic space, evoked only in terms of a proletarian context; and on the other, a different form of "private" space, that of sexuality, of seduction—occurring in the film only as a signifier of bourgeois space.

When a striking worker is arrested through the incriminating evidence of a photograph taken by one of the spies, the boss and a woman companion witness the arrest in the street. Of the two, she reacts the more violently, and screams to kill the worker. Unlike the proletarian couple depicted within domestic space, this couple exists in a more overtly defined sexual space. The woman's clothing and facial expressions are the stereotype of seduction. Hence Eisenstein's use of stereotypes has sexual as well as class dimensions, and the common visual and narrative bond connects the woman and the boss. The young worker's arrest disturbs the enclosed space of the carriage in which the woman and the boss are seated. At the same time, the spectacle of the beating provides a thinly disguised sense of sexual gratification, evocative of the bourgeoise ladies' attack on the young Bolshevik in *October.*

When the same worker signs a confession marking his, and by extension, the workers' downfall, another couple appears, functioning as a rhythmic counterpoint to the scene. A pair of midgets dance the tango on a round dinner table while the worker and police officer sit in the foreground, all four of them facing the camera. The dance provides an almost comic commentary on the worker's confession, and it is this male-female couple which provides the background for the relations of power between police officer and worker. Each of these moments—the worker's arrest and his confession, and the presence of discord in the home life of the workers, signals the breakdown of the strike, and each is accompanied by the appearance of male-female couples, signifiers of private space. That men appear elsewhere in the film, and that women appear only in these contexts marked by discord, suggests that women have, then, a disruptive function in *Strike.*

In the final sequence of the film, the subproles, or "riffraff" as they are referred to in the English titles, infiltrate a workers' march, instigating the final massacre. One of these "unscrupulous men" is a woman who is a parody of the seductive femininity evoked by the boss's companion. The riffraff appear in an underground dwelling, and these scenes recall the representation of private space elsewhere in the film. A man is seen rocking a baby (fig. 2.5), recalling the domestic scene where a man and woman bathe their child (fig. 2.6); and a dwarf assists the leader of these people, reminding the viewer of the tango-dancing couple. When the infiltrators set fire to a liquor store just as the strikers are walking by, attention is focused on the woman. She climbs up a tree and screams (the word "DES-TROY" appears in the English titles), attempting to incite the workers to riot (fig. 2.7). This image is a direct reference to the woman who so enthusiastically screamed for the worker's death from inside the boss's carriage (fig. 2.8). The riffraff live literally underground—an apt depiction of the way in which images of the private sphere appear in this Eisenstein film.[2] The representation of the dwelling and the actions of the riffraff recombine all the elements associated with the representation of private space, whether domestic or sexual, and reduce them to grotesque parody. Here, where the riffraff live, the boundaries between private and public space are destroyed, and this destruction is the flip side of the condensation of signs of private space operative in these scenes. When the police attack the workers, they finally invade their tenements and, at one point, pitch a child from a balcony. The horrific proportions of the conclusion lie partially in the violation of the distinction between private and public space. As agents of narrative resolution, the police literally tear down the meaningful distinctions according to which the film has developed.

Women exist in *Strike* primarily as signifiers of private

Fig.   2.5

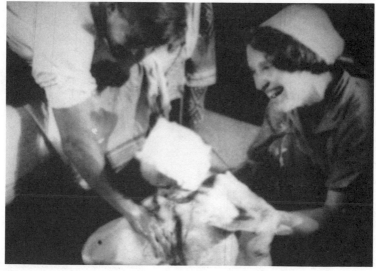

Fig.   2.6

Fig.   2.7

Fig.   2.8

space. The narrative function of private space as an oblique perspective is structurally similar to the roles of the spies and intermediary figures in the film. Through women, as well as through the spies, the central activity of the strike is seen at an indirect angle. The spies represent an access to power through disguise, through image-making, through concealed vision. Women are, whether proletarian or bourgeoise, the vehicles through which strength dissipates. But the women and the spies of *Strike* are alike in that, as the signs of private space on the one hand, and voyeuristic vision on the other, they are, within the narrative logic of the film, displaced perspectives on political relations. To be sure, the activities of the spies and the functions of the women are political in their own right. Indeed, *Strike* displays a tension between conflicting modes of political formation. First, there is the rigid hierarchy of primary (boss versus worker) and secondary contradictions (male versus female, social versus domestic space), a hierarchy corresponding to a classical, even if excessively mechanistic, Marxist view. Then there is a notion of opposition where class allegiances do not function as the supreme and unique mode of signification, where the very decidability of class as a clear-cut entity is put into question, where women, the spies, and the riffraff become representations of the difficulty of a simple binary opposition. It is too simple, I think, to describe Eisenstein as a filmmaker in whose work the political and the aesthetic would often collide. Far more significant are the kinds of political and aesthetic factors at work, and the fact that there is no single notion of "the" political or "the" aesthetic with which to form a neat duality. Rather, it is opposition itself which assumes different representations in *Strike,* and those representations cut across the boundaries that separate the political from the aesthetic.

The close affinities, both historical and thematic, between *Strike* and Eisenstein's theatrical experience are relevant in this context.[3] In particular, it was through *Strike* that Eisenstein defined *montage of attractions,* a definition which emerged, precisely, from the theater. The attraction is the most basic unit of those theatrical devices which elicit a particular emotional response from the viewer/spectator: " . . . every element that brings to light in the spectator those senses or that psychology that influence his experience—every element that can be verified and mathematically calculated to produce certain emotional shocks in a proper order within the totality . . ."[4] Montage of attractions is an early formulation of Eisenstein's stress on montage as collision, and the most apparent instances of the principle in *Strike* show the influence of theater, and in particular of the circus: the equation of the spies to animals, the tango-dancing couple. These allusions to the circus become, in *Strike,* commentaries on the corrupt power of capitalism. At the same time they illustrate the tension that exists in *Strike* between different conceptions of opposition, for these eruptions of the grotesque, of the bestial, are also moments of fascination that threaten to upset the division of the world into opposing camps of normal and abnormal, human and animal.

In a discussion of *Strike,* Stephen Crofts says that the various aesthetic strategies of the film—the grotesque allusions, the disruption of linear development, the refusal to designate any of the actors in the film as "characters" in the traditional sense—serve to illustrate Eisenstein's "radical conception of montage as a principle of fragmentation, heterogeneity and appeal to the spectator to make conceptual connections clearly . . ."[5] After the horrendous massacre of workers that forms the concluding episode of *Strike,* extreme close-ups of wide-open eyes are intercut with titles admonishing proletarians to remember. This conclusion would indeed suggest that the wide-eyed, direct apprehension of the past is to be seen in direct opposition to the various forms of vision—peeking, spying, and otherwise surreptitiously intruding—that have characterized the enemies of the proletariat. However, I am not convinced that spectatorship as it is elaborated in *Strike* can be so readily broken down into two opposing camps. If the close-ups of the eyes are suggestive of the strategies that have been used throughout the film to convey the opposition of bosses and workers, they are equally suggestive, in their wide-eyed fascination, of the position of the voyeur. I have argued already that *Strike* is characterized by a tension between different notions of opposition. That tension may not necessarily negate Crofts's claims that the spectator is encouraged to "make conceptual connections clearly," but it does put into question the attendant implication that spectatorship, as it is elaborated in the film, serves a clearly defined political purpose. Rather, the spectator addressed by *Strike* is addressed in heterogeneous terms. Now I do not take this to mean that *Strike* is, therefore, a film in which the free play of the signifier puts the coherence of the signified into question, thereby articulating a cinematic *écriture* of the refusal of rigid binary oppositions. Rather, the tension which I have described in *Strike* is symptomatic of an extremely limited hetereogeneity, limited precisely by the boundaries of gender.

Put another way, the figure of woman in *Strike* marks the undecidability of boundaries. On one level, women function as mediators between private and public space in the sense that they appear in the film in order to designate the private sphere as a realm both distinct from and connected to the public sphere of capitalist society. The private, domestic sphere is the spatial equivalent of the oblique vision represented by the spies. But woman in *Strike* takes on a rather particular function in this respect. Within the logic of the film, women may well be creatures of their class, but as *women* they are defined by something other than class at the same time. If the spies function as mediators between workers and bosses, there is never any question whose side they serve. Women, however, constitute ambiguity personified; the category of sex is introduced in *Strike* in such a way as to put the absolute boundaries between classes into question. While it does not require too much imagination to read this ambiguity as the symptom of a none-too-ambiguous sexism, my purpose is not to indict Eisenstein, or Soviet cinema for that matter, for his/its waffling engagement with the woman question. I would argue, rather, that the figure of woman in *Strike* demonstrates, better than virtually any other aspect of the film, how the collision and conflict so central to Eisenstein's theory and practice of montage is undermined by a tension that cannot be so easily or readily resolved into opposing forces. Hence, the characteristic strategies of *Strike*—the operations of defamiliarization and fragmentation—do not serve a precisely defined, coherent, ideological end. What gives *Strike* its particular shape and resonance is the ambiguity with which narrative opposition is created. At the same time that the film seems to want to reproduce a world in which male and female, public and private, are distinctly separate entities, the very forms that convey those oppositions are themselves suggestive of the breakdown of firm barriers.

Women signify the two kinds of private space represented in the film—one with primarily domestic and familial connotations, the other with more sexual ones. In this sense, women evoke what is repressed or otherwise removed from center stage in the public sphere. The eyes seen at the conclusion of *Strike* suggest both the distance *and* the affinity between the differing modes of vision that have been represented—one ostensibly bourgeois, the other ostensibly proletarian. If woman serves as a signifier of the private sphere, she also acquires a function in relationship to spectatorship as it is represented in the film. The woman accompanying the boss, who watches the worker's arrest with great glee, observes the scene from the vantage point of a spectator, and thus recalls the position of the spies; she also functions as a link between that intermediary position and the one occupied by the police, since she clearly is excited by the possibility of violence. The caricature of this woman, who appears during the infiltration of the worker's march, similarly is linked to the intermediary functions of the spies as well as the police. The boundary separating these women, representatives of bourgeois order, from the women in the film who clearly are designated as proletarian, is weak indeed. For virtually all of the female figures in *Strike* are connected by their common status as signifiers of discord.

The disruptive function of women as signifiers of the private sphere in *Strike* recalls Lenin's comments (reported by Clara Zetkin) on the potentially reactionary function of women in revolutionary struggle:

Very few husbands, not even the proletarians, think of how much they could lighten the burdens and worries of their wives, or relieve them entirely, if they lent a hand in this "women's work." But no, that would go against the "privilege and dignity of the husband." He demands that he have rest and comfort. The domestic life of the woman is a daily sacrifice of self to a thousand insignificant trifles. The ancient rights of her husband, her lord and master, survive unnoticed. Objectively, his slave takes her revenge. Also in concealed form. Her backwardness and her lack of understanding for her husband's revolutionary ideals act as a drag on his fighting spirit, on his determination to fight. They are like tiny worms, gnawing and undermining imperceptibly, slowly but surely.[6]

Eisenstein's representation of the private sphere in *Strike* draws upon the kind of apprehension expressed by Lenin in this passage. On the surface, Lenin's observations suggest that unless the equation between private and female, male and public is challenged, then an inevitable drain on revolutionary energy will occur. However, the extent of that challenge is not clear, for revolutionary energy appears to be defined quite emphatically in male terms. To be sure, Lenin calls for an end to women's domestic slavery, but the attendant implications of what that end would mean in terms of a socialist conception of the private and the public remain undefined.

One of Eisenstein's unrealized projects was the filming of Marx's *Capital,* a project described in Eisenstein's notebooks in 1927 and 1928. Annette Michelson has noted that in his project for a film of *Capital,* Eisenstein attempted to rethink *Strike,* particularly insofar as the political activity represented in the film has little or no economic motivation.[7] Eisenstein's notes for a film of *Capital* also suggest a continuing preoccupation with the representation of private life and sexual polarity. Hence, Eisenstein describes an episode which might serve as a basis for "visual instruction in the dialectical method":

I.e., just as the "house-wifely virtues" of a German worker's wife constitute the greatest evil, the strongest obstacle to a revolutionary uprising, given the German context. A German worker's wife will always have something warm for her husband, will never let him go completely hungry. And there is the root of her negative role which slows the pace of social development.[8]

In Lenin's formulation it is suppressed anger and rebellion that cause the woman to be a reactionary presence; in Eisenstein's, it is rather, the fact that the woman performs her traditional role so well. If revolutionary fervor seems to have male connotations in Lenin's view, one wonders if the "pace of social development" to which Eisenstein refers is synonymous, too, with male development.

I surely would be accused of stating the obvious, however, if I were to conclude that *Strike* is symptomatic of a tendency to articulate "revolutionary" and "male" as synonymous terms. My point, rather, is that while the figure of woman may well be evoked in order to suggest her "negative role," her presence has far-reaching effects on the narrative and visual structure of the film. One of the most important functions of montage, as defined and theorized by Eisenstein as well as other Soviet filmmakers of the period, is the creation of cinematic metaphors. The function of metaphors in film, and in Soviet film of the 1920s in particular, where montage is used in such a way as to create far-reaching metaphors, has been somewhat perplexing. In Roman Jakobson's famous definition, metaphor and metonymy stem from the two axes of linguistic organization—the paradigmatic axis, or that of selection, in the case of metaphor, and the syntagmatic axis, or that of contiguity, in the case of metonymy. While Jakobson did suggest, briefly, the relevance of the operations of metaphor and metonymy to film (with examples drawn, respectively, from Charlie Chaplin and D. W. Griffith), recent discussions of metaphor and metonymy have emphasized, rather, the extent to which the two operations are mutually interdependent in film. The comparisons of the spies to the animals whose names they bear in *Strike,* for instance, seem to be rather pure examples of cinematic metaphor, and the dissolves that create the link between the faces of the men and the faces of the animals a fairly obvious equivalent for the implicit "like" or "as" of metaphor. However, prior to these dissolves, one of the spies is first introduced in an animal store, and this more immediate connection with the diegesis of the film suggests metonymy.[9] The analogy drawn between the slaughter of the workers and the slaughter of animals at the film's conclusion seems, likewise, to be a fairly pure example of cinematic metaphor, drawing in this case upon alternating montage for its creation. But the metaphor does evoke the earlier scene where mounted police attack a workers' meeting in the woods, so that the analogy is inserted, at least partially, within the diegetic context of the film, particularly concerning the association between animals and aggression. Hence, once again, a seemingly obvious instance of cinematic metaphor also can be seen to function as cinematic metonymy.

As I've suggested, in chapter one, the figure of woman in Soviet film of the 1920s does not correspond readily to the poles of metaphor and metonymy, even when they are defined as interdependent, since woman's ambivalent role is to be, simultaneously, on both sides of metaphoric and metonymic relations. Put another way, the figure of woman puts into question not only the distinction between metaphor and metonymy, but the distinction between the figural and diegetic levels of the text upon which the very notion of metaphor and metonymy depends, as well. Montage may well function to destabilize the relationship between internal and external, diegetic and nondiegetic elements of the narrative. Crofts says of this destabilizing function of montage that "[w]ithin and between shots there is an incessant agitation and dynamism whose role can often be diegetic—the gathering momentum of the strike, for instance—but is throughout the film percussive, denying the spectator the false repose of a false illusion of continuity."[10] The most frequently cited uses of metaphor and metonymy in *Strike* invoke the analogy between reactionary force and the animal world (the analogy between the spies and the animals; the comparison of the slaughter of workers to the slaughter of animals), or the representation of the brute force of the capitalists (the demonstration of the juicer, coinciding with the attack by mounted police). In these examples, the distinction between what is proper to the narrative of the film and what is external to it breaks down. But there is a much more radical breakdown of another order. It is not only the metaphoric elements in *Strike* which put into question the distinction between the diegetic and the nondiegetic. The figure of woman exemplifies the ambivalent status of simultaneous centrality and marginality, now a functional element of a narrative dynamic, now an excessive rhetorical flourish.

3. *Mother* and Son

PART OF what is interesting about Eisenstein's *Strike,* in the context of Soviet cinema of the 1920s and the woman question, is that the film is not obviously or explicitly concerned with gender or sexuality. However, it becomes clear upon close examination that the narrative development of the film relies crucially on the connections made between different kinds of intermediaries, whether they be the boss's emissaries who spy on the workers, or the women who figure as disruptions of unity in the strike activity. In contrast, Pudovkin's 1926 film, *Mother,* is perhaps the most obvious film of the period to consider under the rubric of Soviet film and the woman question. Pudovkin's film traces the increasing politicization of a woman as she moves from an identity defined exclusively in patriarchal terms to an identity shaped by commitment to political struggle. The film suggests that women's traditional roles, and particularly as they concern motherhood, can be redefined dialectically; that is, that what constitutes the oppression of women also can constitute their emancipation. However, the way in which this process of emancipation evolves in Pudovkin's film calls into question the extent to which emancipation is a rewriting of patriarchy, rather than a challenge to it.

Maxim Gorky's novel *Mother* was published in 1907. It has been described as the single most important work to define what would eventually be called socialist realism in the Soviet Union.[1] Gorky's novel tells the story of an elderly widow who, primarily through the revolutionary activity of her son Pavel, develops political consciousness, and moves away from traditional religious values. Quite simply, Gorky's novel tells the story of the necessity for socialist consciousness. The novel is straightforward in its realism, relatively simple in its presentation, and traditional in format. "Traditional," that is, in the sense that *Mother* takes the basic structure of the Western middle-class novel and substitutes socialist content. Gorky's novel represents the simplest—and perhaps most simplistic—definition of a dialectical approach to art, for the traditional novel is understood here as problematic, in socialist terms, only insofar as its content is concerned. This simplicity is not without problems. The mother's change is presented as an alternative to a religion-based existence, yet that change has all the trappings of a religious conversion. In particular, her son Pavel takes on a function that it is entirely appropriate to describe as Christ-like. This leaves the distinct impression that the religious framework is a way of making socialist ideals more palatable. As a result, the socialist consciousness of the novel has a profoundly religious quality.

Pudovkin's 1926 film is based quite loosely on the Gorky novel. The religious context so central to the novel virtually disappears. The father, dead from the outset in the novel, is an important figure in the film, until his death begins the chain of events leading to the mother's transformation. Screenwriter Nathan Zarkhy explained that the basic theme of the film was taken from Gorky's novel, while "the course of the story and of the characters is developed independently of the novel . . ."[2] More specifically, the scenario of the Pudovkin film is based on actual events which occurred in 1905 and 1906, some of which had been published as reminiscences in *Pravda*.[3] The film *Mother,* then, is a product of the intersection between fiction and historical document so central to the development of Soviet narrative film. If *Strike* condenses many events and theoretical points in an obliquely structured narrative that refers to many incidents without referring to any specific ones, *Mother* is a reading of a political novel via actual political events.

Even while recognizing the limits of the relationship between the film and the novel, it would be a mistake to dismiss the Gorky source as irrelevant, despite the fact that Pudovkin's film is not an adaptation in the strict sense. The film bears Gorky's signature, in much the same way as Kuleshov's *By the Law* bears London's signature. This is not to say that Gorky's name appears to assure, simply and facilely, the political correctness of the film. Rather, Pudovkin's film reexamines the historical potential of the novel from the cinematic angle. Gorky's novel is, already, such an examination, a rendering of the traditional novel format in terms of revolutionary consciousness. Pudovkin submits the traditional form, and Gorky's use of it, to scrutiny.

Somewhat like *Strike, Mother* presents an oblique perspective on political consciousness: the perspective of those outside of production, and outside of political life in general. Whereas women in *Strike* occupy marginal but nonetheless significant positions, *Mother* takes the relationship between women and revolutionary change as its central subject. The elderly woman suddenly is exposed to revolutionary consciousness when her husband and her son clash in a struggle that results in her husband's death. The son is arrested for his political activities, and the mother unwittingly betrays him, naively believing that telling the authorities the truth will set him free. At Pavel's trial, the mother suddenly reacts to both the injustice done her son, and the many years of her own suffering. He is sent to jail, and the mother begins working with the revolutionaries. An escape plan for Pavel initially succeeds, but both mother and son are killed by mounted police at the very moment they are reunited.

The narrative structure of *Mother* revolves around the pivotal scene of Pavel's trial, which marks the mother's sudden change in vision and understanding. During the first part of the film, leading up to the trial, there is a constant play between interior and exterior space. The mother is seen only within the confines of the home, of domestic space. The remaining interiors are public contexts: the bar where Vlasov, the father, tries unsuccessfully to exchange a flatiron (used as a weight on a clock in the home) for a drink, and where he joins the "Black Hundreds," the mercenaries who immediately see him as "someone we could use"; the factory, only briefly perceived from within; and the police station, also glimpsed briefly. In all of these interior spaces, a sense of oppressive force reigns. It is only within the home, however, that such force is perceived from the standpoint of the victim. Oppressive force is also dominant in the exterior shots of the first part of the film. The second shot shows a Czarist police officer strolling in front of a bar, as if to claim that the public sphere is his domain. When factory exteriors are represented, they provide a context for the pursuit of the revolutionaries by the mercenaries. The only visual alternative to this oppressive atmosphere occurs prior to the factory demonstration, when the revolutionaries meet secretly in the woods. A brief series of establishing shots conveys the realm of nature as a distinct counterpoint to what has been seen thus far. In addition, this space is a privileged realm to which only the revolutionaries have access.[4]

The first image of the mother shows her performing household labor. Although her oppression is established, the image also conveys relative calm. This calm is disturbed, first by the arrival of her drunken husband with whom she struggles over the clock; and a second time, after the husband's death, by the police officers who come into the house to question Pavel, where the alternation of medium-shot and close-up creates an

Fig. 3.1

especially vivid representation of oppressive hierarchy (figs. 3.1 and 3.2). These forms of patriarchal authority—the family and the state—intrude upon the mother's space in essentially the same way: by force. Pavel also intrudes upon this space, although in a qualitatively different way. Early in the film, Pavel agrees to hide some guns in the house, which he conceals under floorboards as the mother, who is ostensibly asleep, watches dimly through half-closed eyes. This is a less violent intrusion, and the mother herself will later imitate Pavel's gesture when she begins working with the revolutionaries.

The turning point is Pavel's trial, and there is a basic rhyming structure between the scenes preceding and following the trial. In the latter half of the film, indoor and outdoor space contrast, as in the first half of the film. Pavel is in prison, while militant activity develops outside the prison walls; earlier in the film, his mother also was captured in the metaphoric

Fig.   3.2

prison of the home. And just as the prison is an extreme
representation of the imprisonment of the mother within the
home, so the political consciousness shown in the second half
of the film is much more developed than the dispersed leaflet-
ing and meetings seen in the first part.

   Mother also can be understood as an attempt to redefine the
very nature of motherhood. Absolute devotion to her son
motivates the mother to cooperate naively and unthinkingly
with the police. Yet, this devotion is hardly reducible to simplistic cooptation with the reactionary forces. On the one
hand, and especially during the first part of the film, motherhood is a suffocating, self-enclosed relationship. On the
other hand, and specifically during the second half, motherhood is presented as transcending these limited boundaries
to make connections with other realms of experience. In
Pudovkin's film, the mother's transformation is, precisely, the
movement from one kind of mother relationship to the other.

   Woman represents, then, the unpoliticized. Motherhood
becomes a grand metaphor for the process whereby revolu-

tionary consciousness transforms the privatized, fragmented relationship—in which the mother unwittingly betrays her son because she has virtually no connection to the social universe—into, precisely, a social relationship. Motherhood becomes a support for participation in collective action and collective consciousness, rather than a force working against them. Since the overt conflict in the film is between these two conceptions of motherhood—one private and isolated, the other social and communal—the relationship between the private and the public is central. In *Mother,* the separation between private and public space appears on two levels. First, there is a tension between interior and exterior space, and second, there is a difference between a fragmented, isolated view of motherhood and a collective view. The separation between private and public space is central to both the dynamics of narrative and of revolutionary consciousness.

Yet, contrary to what one might expect, in the second part of the film, after Pavel's trial, and after the mother has begun to define herself as a social being, domestic space is not redefined in relation to the public sphere. Rather, it is obliterated. Only once does the interior space of the home appear again after Pavel's trial. This is when the mother hides political leaflets—rather than guns—under the floorboards. Here, the home appears primarily to recall the original image of the concealed guns and to drain it of its significance as a threat to the mother. This obliteration of domestic space would seem to suggest that the development of political consciousness is a unilateral movement outwards, functioning in broader and broader social terms. Domestic space becomes unimportant per se, or perhaps completely synonymous with social space; in either case, domestic space no longer has a place within the mother's consciousness, nor within the figural and metaphoric structure of the film.

There is another woman present in *Mother* who has an

important narrative function in relation to this obliteration of domestic space. This is the lone female revolutionary who brings the guns for Pavel to hide. She is present at Pavel's trial, and she is a key participant in the escape attempt from the prison, during which she and Pavel are separated.[5] The woman's function is secondarily as a revolutionary; she is first and foremost a potential love interest that is never realized. Heterosexual coupledom is displaced, in other words, by the mother-son relationship. Pavel's relationship with the woman already has a political dimension, and so the mother-son relationship becomes primal, in political as well as emotional terms. The son is returned to his mother in a gesture which integrates the realms of family ties and social activism.

The most decisive stage in the mother's change in consciousness is the trial. The sequence of the trial begins with a series of images of the courthouse exterior. Pavel enters the courthouse. Inside, the mother sits alone as observers begin to enter the courtroom (fig. 3.3). Before the trial begins, the judges are shown in their chambers. They are three fools: one is distinctly vain, the second can barely stay awake, and the third is captivated by a picture of his horse, at which he constantly glances throughout the trial. As the trial begins, several spectators in the courtroom notice the presence of Pavel's mother (fig. 3.4). One spectator in particular stands out: a well-dressed, obviously bourgeoise woman wearing a lorgnette who stares at the mother as if she were a freak at a sideshow, and who comments on the trial as if chatting about friends over tea ("the presiding judge is so nice, isn't he," one title says) (figs. 3.5 and 3.6).

At the beginning of the trial there are three sets of intertwined reactions. The woman with the lorgnette is visibly entertained by the whole process; the judges are bored; and the mother by this point has been driven to tears. The trial itself is presented as a bad joke, as a travesty of justice. Pavel's

Fig.   3.3

Fig.   3.4

lawyer is drunk, and his defense is hardly coherent. Pavel is
sentenced to hard labor in Siberia. Again, different reactions
are juxtaposed. The woman puts away her lorgnette, for the
show is over; Pavel's comrades are obviously relieved that no
death sentence was imposed; and the mother, for the first

Fig. 3.5   Fig. 3.6

time, responds aggressively. She suddenly stands up screaming "Where is truth?" She rushes toward Pavel and asks his
forgiveness. Meanwhile, the judges have returned to their
chambers, where the one returns to a more eager contemplation of his horse.

It is significant, I think, that the most decisive step in the
mother's radical change is accompanied by these particular
courtroom theatrics. There are two sets of relationships in
the courtroom scene: between Pavel and the judges (that is,
between the forces of revolution and those of the state), on
the one hand, and between the mother and the lorgnetted
woman, on the other. The mother's response to the trial, first
as a helpless victim and then as an angry mother, is portrayed against the backdrop of the bourgeoise woman's
response. If the scene is divided in this way, between male
and female responses, it is to suggest that the woman with
the lorgnette represents a position that may not be exactly
the same as that of the judges, but which supports their
power. This woman, as a spectator, embodies a detached
amusement which, the film suggests, is just as much a function of female socialization as the mother's obedient attitude
toward her husband and toward the police. Indeed, the
lorgnetted woman represents another form of obedience, for
she notes with approval the demeanor of the judges. At the
same time, this scene is an acting-out of class hierarchy; the

woman with the lorgnette responds not only as a woman, but as a woman of privilege.

The trial scene recalls two previous scenes. One which immediately precedes the trial, when the mother tells the police officers where the guns are hidden, is a similarly structured encounter with official authority. In that scene, the mother's response to the authority of the police officers is obedience carried to the extreme; she repeatedly bows to them. Then, in the trial scene, the authority figures have become caricatures. What the mother sees for the first time are relations of force and of power, in part because she herself is powerless to effect any action whatsoever. In this context, the woman with the lorgnette acquires another significant function; she suggests an alternative way to accept powerlessness—through detached amusement and observation. Of course, the mother was equally powerless in the previous scene, although she imagined herself to have at least some control. Suddenly, the authority of the police and the judges is revealed to the mother as nothing more than spectacle. This occurs primarily through the courtroom observers, especially the lorgnetted woman, for whom the participants in a life and death situation are simply actors, and the trial is a pageant performed for their benefit.

Since the primary spectator on whom attention is focused is a woman, she—like the mother and the female revolutionary—has as her major function responsiveness and receptivity. And since the women in *Strike* function to signify the margins of strike activity per se, there is a connection between these two films in that both designate female figures as representing what lies outside of the realm of capitalist and state power per se. The lorgnetted woman responds to the trial in a personalized fashion, speaking of the judges as her friends, and regarding the entire event as amusement. She represents a personalized view of established power, just as the woman revolutionary represents a personalized view of the relations between comrades. At the trial, the mother is symbolically located between these two women: one woman on the side of the state, the other on the side of the revolutionaries. If woman is a signifier of the personal, of affective bonds, then the lorgnetted woman represents the degradation of the personal into purely individual gratification, while the woman revolutionary represents a still-unrealized potential for a definition of the political and the personal as integrated. It is only when the mother chooses to identify her love for her son with, rather than against, his revolutionary activities that—the film asks its audience to believe—such potential is realized.

The mother's reaction—"where is truth?" according to the English titles—recalls the beginning of the film, when the mother struggles with Vlasov over the clock. The mother reacted out of her desire to protect the sanctity of domestic space. Similarly, the mother's response at the trial is a spontaneous reaction to patriarchal authority, spurred by the desire to protect the sanctity of a parent-child relationship against the corruption visible in the courtroom. It is impossible to say that the mother suddenly has a full awareness of oppressive, reactionary authority. However, the abrupt switch from the domain of the home to that of the courtroom, where the same power relations exist on a larger scale, allows the mother to make a connection between the power of the father and the power of the state.

In Pudovkin's film, the trial scene is the most striking addition to the events described in Gorki's novel. Whereas some of the scenes are drawn from reminiscences in *Pravda,* the trial scene is adapted from the trial in L. N. Tolstoy's last novel, *Resurrection.*[6] In Tolstoy's novel, a murder trial brings together two people who have not seen each other for many years: the defendant, a woman prostitute on trial for poisoning a man, and a member of the jury, a nobleman whose seduction and abandonment of that woman many years before marked the beginning of her life as a prostitute. The novel opens with the trial, which proceeds much in the same way as Pavel's trial. The judges are bored and restless (one of them is preoccupied with his "Swiss girlfriend"), and the defense is unprepared. Against this background of a parody of justice, the nobleman, Nekhludov, begins to question drastically his own life once he recognizes the woman, Katusha. He sees in her both a reflection of his own past and a symbol of his own responsibility— or lack of it. The trial initiates, in short, a radical change of consciousness in Nekhludov: "The terrible veil, which for ten years had hung between him and the consequence of his crime, was beginning to waver, and now and again he caught a glimpse of what was hidden behind it."[7] Such also is the significance of Pavel's trial for the mother. The parallel "crime" in her past is her betrayal of her son, and the trial has a similar narrative significance in *Mother* and in Tolstoy's novel. It is a public ritual in which the emergence of an unexpected feature—the recognition of authoritarian figures as buffoons, or the appearance of a person from one's own past—provokes change. The trial scene as it is brought to the screen in *Mother* represents a moment of fusion between the home and the public sphere, between Pavel as his mother's child and Pavel as a revolutionary. The trial marks the beginning of such connections for the mother. As Richard Taylor puts it, the events in the courtroom "bring the mother from passive acquiescence in the old world to active participation in the struggle for the new."[8] The narrative function of the trial, in this respect, is not unlike the birthday party in *By the Law,* a similar moment of mediation between private and public selves. In each film, a socialist author—London, Gorky—is adapted to the screen via detours through a novelistic tradition represented by Dostoevsky and Tolstoy.

Even though domestic space no longer is depicted on the

screen once the mother has begun to become politically aware, the relationship between mother and son intensifies. In other words, their relationship truly flourishes when it moves beyond the privatized space of the home. Within the home, the son defends his mother against the tyrant father; but in the social sphere, he defends his class against an entire system. The mother's role in this process is ultimately that of intermediary, both in terms of Pavel's relationship, as a revolutionary, to family and state authority, and in terms of the viewer's perception of that very process. While *Mother* appears to be a film that is identified with the perspective of the mother, since it is her change that gives the film its basic structure, the overarching perspective of the film is clearly identified with the son. It is *his* revolution, and *his* identity that ultimately benefits from the change in the mother. That Pavel is meant to stand for revolutionary Soviet society only reinforces this role. It does not require too much imagination to see the film as profoundly oedipal in this sense. To be sure, some of the dimensions of the oedipal conflict have been adapted to socialist ends—it is the son who represents a new symbolic order, replacing the corrupt and outmoded order of the father; and the mother-child bond serves the socialist public sphere. However much the film distinguishes between the power of the father and the power of the son, thereby suggesting that the patriarchal order which oppresses the mother would disappear under the socialist regime, it is nonetheless male power which reigns supreme. To be sure, the film creates a utopian vision of male and female unity. But that utopian vision is undone by the fact that such unity can only be a function of such a profoundly oedipal vision of the world, where the possible equality between men and women is circumscribed by the bond between mother and son. Indeed, women are only significant in *Mother* to the extent that they embody nurturing roles. Even the relatively minor figures, such as Pavel's comrade and the lorgnetted woman in the courtroom, function as mirrors held up to men, whether the men in question are revolutionaries or reactionaries. In this context, it is important to recall how we first see Pavel on the screen: not as an active revolutionary, but as a mother's child, sleeping in the corner of the house and awakened by his father's violence. The child grows up in the course of the film. While the mother's change is the ostensible center of the film, she remains above and beyond all else a mother.

Perhaps, it could be argued that Pudovkin's film only reflects the reigning ideology of his time concerning the sanctity of motherhood. Even individuals such as Alexandra Kollontai, who insisted continually on the importance of sexual politics in socialist change, designated motherhood as a special area of consideration: " . . . the woman's responsibilities towards the social collective, society, will always be somewhat different to men's. The woman is not only an independent worker and citizen—at the same time she is a mother, a bearer of the future."9

However, in Pudovkin's film, the mother is not an independent worker and citizen *at the same time* that she is a mother. Rather, she is a social being only *because* she is a mother. In any case, I would argue that despite the overt preoccupation with motherhood, the film is engaged more with motherhood as a symptom than as a concern in its own right. Motherhood is symptomatic of the tension, in Soviet society of the 1920s, concerning women's positions as subjects within socialism. The revision of the marriage laws in 1926 was initiated in order to protect women who had been victimized by the marriage laws that took effect immediately after the revolution. The protection of women was assured, however, by reinforcing a husband's traditional role as provider and caretaker. Kollontai's position was that socialism should provide for all citizens, who should be sexual equals in this respect. In a 1918

pamphlet she discusses the divorce laws, whereby women as
well as men could file for divorce in a simple civil ceremony:

Women who are unhappy in their married life welcome this easy
divorce. But others, particularly those who are used to looking
upon their husband as "breadwinners," are frightened. They have
not yet understood that a woman must accustom herself to seek
and find support in the collective and in society, and not from the
individual man.[10]

The risk in positing the collective and society as substitutes for
the forms of authority that women have found traditionally
within the family is in perpetuating a patriarchal structure, in
substituting one father figure for another. At the very least, in
Kollontai's writings, these issues are addressed from the point
of view of women. In Pudovkin's film, the woman's point of
view is subterfuge. The film sidesteps the question of patriarchal authority by focusing on the son rather than the father,
thereby making the woman a function of the son's rebellion
against, simultaneously, the forces of familial and governmen-
tal authority.

If motherhood is women's access to revolutionary consciousness in Pudovkin's film, it also is suggested that revolutionary bonds are as natural as the link between mother and
son. Political consciousness is seen as a natural process whereby, in the most famous scene of the film, the growing consciousness of masses of people is equated to the breaking-up
of ice floes with the advent of spring. And so, the uprising of
the people is seen as an event as natural as the four seasons,
and as natural as a mother's love for her son.

Nature is introduced as a visual motif in the film through
images of water, which function at first as background elements. Gradually, in the course of the film, they are foregrounded and acquire a metaphoric status. When the revolutionaries are first presented, their meeting in the woods is

preceded by establishing shots of trees and a brook. Here, nature functions to define an alternative space to the enclosed, claustrophobic space of the home and the bar. The signifier of water evolves through several stages and detours, before becoming a metaphor at the conclusion of the film for the awakening "spring" of the masses. When a man is beaten by the Black Hundreds, images of water form a counterpoint. Images of the man being beaten are intercut with images of water, now moving more rapidly than in the previous shots of a brook. Water also functions in this contrapuntal way within the home. The mother stares fixedly at slowly dripping water while her dead husband lies in the house. In both of these instances, the counterpoint stems from the primarily diegetic function of the water. During the attack on the man, for example, we know that the brook exists close by the factory, even though it has not been seen in the context of the factory; and we know that the water at which the mother stares exists within the house. This development of contrapuntal imagery resembles the way in which the musicians, during the bar scene where the father is recruited to the Black Hundreds, are first used to establish simply the ambiance of the bar. As the same images of them appear throughout the sequence, however, they begin to function as a commentary on the discourse of the mercenaries.

A famous scene from the film also shows water as an element of Pavel's joy when he discovers, in a note delivered by his mother, that an escape plan is in the works. Pavel's happy facial expression is juxtaposed to images of a babbling brook and a cheerful baby. This metaphor does not simply signify "joy" through a juncture of images with certain cultural connotations. Pavel's joy is conveyed by a reorganization of previously seen images of the physical universe (water) and of human nature (the baby, suggesting the parent-child relationship), thereby combining the metaphoric and metonymic registers of the film. Unlike Eisenstein's *Strike,* however, Pudovkin's metaphors tend to lean much more heavily toward metonymy; in this sense, the representational universe of *Mother* is much more enclosed than that of *Strike.* Pavel's mother brings him good news, and the filmic representation of his response sets up the mother-child relationship as the point of contact between political consciousness and human relations.

The final use of water as metaphor—the equation of the demonstrating masses with ice floes breaking up on the river—also is situated firmly within a diegetic context. Pavel, escaped from prison, attempts to dodge the police on the ice floes. Once he has rejoined the demonstrators, the breaking ice floes are seen in counterpoint to the marchers. The movement of human beings is inscribed as part of a natural cycle. But it is finally Pavel who is given the most direct access to these images of nature. His revolutionary activity marks the introduction of water imagery at the beginning of the film; his revolutionary activity marks its presence—on a broader scale—at the film's conclusion. Pavel's joy is represented in the film by a leap into another sphere of imagery, the most metaphorical figures in the film. His mother's joy, in contrast, is signified by a very limited figural field—the sight of him. The water imagery constitutes the work of metaphor in the immediate sense in the film. Woman, as mother, constitutes another kind of metaphor: she is the point of access between the human individual and the natural cycles within which *his* activity is inscribed. Ultimately, then, *Mother* is not the mother's film; it is Pavel's.

Nature, understood as the mother-child relationship on the one hand, and the rhythm of seasonal changes on the other, is the key term throughout the development of *Mother.* If domestic space is obliterated in the film, social activity is inscribed within the laws of nature. And even though *Mother* departs significantly from the Gorky novel, the role of nature in the film is not unlike the religious imagery that so dominates the novel. Pudovkin's *Mother* is a simplistic appropriation of cinematic narrative to socialist ends. Like *Strike, Mother* develops a complex system of metaphor based on simultaneous movements of textual resonance and expanding connotative registers. However, the use of metaphor in *Mother* posits nature, not as an iconographic system, and not as a realm in constant interaction with the social activities of human beings; but rather as a fixed reference point, an unchanging, mystified realm. A mother's relationship to her son is presented as the very essence of female identity—when sons have committed themselves to revolutionary change, the film suggests, mothers will soon follow. Cinematic metaphor here does not posit ambiguously the field of binary oppositions, as is the case in *Strike;* it reproduces them with a vengeance. Reproduction and revolutionary activity are the means by which humans—divided into the opposing categories of mothers and sons—have access to that privileged realm. *Strike* does not make such pretensions to the natural world; Eisenstein's film focuses, rather, on the connections between various forms of marginality, and on the connections between social relations and vision itself. In place of this critical process, *Mother* extends an invitation to its audience to share in a ritualistic affirmation of the natural rightness of socialist consciousness. *Mother* is undoubtedly a more "successful" socialist film, if by successful is meant its subservience to a rigid political formula. Indeed, *Mother* was something of a rarity, a film which received unqualified success when it was first shown in the Soviet Union.[11] Official success does not obscure, however, the price paid for ideological coherence. For *Mother* relies, obsessively and passionately, on the links between a socialist view of the world and the realm of nature posited as truth. Unfortunately, such passion and obsession require the continuation of an oedipal narrative form which can only repeat the very law of the father that this film purports to reject.

4. *Bed and Sofa* and the Edge of Domesticity

IN *STRIKE,* domestic space occupies a significant but marginalized position in the narrative of the film; and even though *Mother* is ostensibly about a woman's experiences, there is no further representation of domestic space on the screen after her political awakening. Abram Room's 1927 film, *Bed and Sofa,* is centrally and explicitly concerned with domestic life. Unlike the evocations of the revolutionary past in *Strike* and *Mother, Bed and Sofa* deals with everyday life after the revolution. Hence, while it is obviously the case that all Soviet films reveal something of the political climate in which they were made, *Bed and Sofa* offers a unique opportunity to examine how the woman question is posed in a film that reflects quite directly upon contemporary events, and particularly as they affect women's lives and male-female relationships. The everyday life evoked in the film touches upon a number of issues, such as marriage, monogamy, everyday sexism, abortion, and female autonomy. *Bed and Sofa* is especially interesting as a contradictory text. Like *Mother,* the film suggests motherhood as the most basic component of female self-determination; but unlike Pudovkin's film, there is less of a clear-cut metaphorical agenda associated with motherhood. Rather, *Bed and Sofa* raises a number of narrative and ideological questions that it is unable, or unwilling, to answer.

Bed and Sofa is unlike most of the films considered the "classics" of Soviet silent film in its subject matter as well as in its style. A reviewer for *Close Up* even described the film as characterized by "reckless cuts, by unrelated continuity, by every fault that the amateur can make." The reviewer continues: "And yet here was a film that gripped and had genius. Its very uneven-ness gave it an odd power; almost, one might say, created a new technique."[1] *Bed and Sofa* is less characteristic than other films of the montage style so typical of Soviet films of the 1920s. Yet, even though the film does not rely on montage in the same accentuated way as the films of other directors during this period, *Bed and Sofa* nonetheless uses montage in a more subtle way to explore the overlapping relationships between men and women, and private and public life, in the new socialist society.

Bed and Sofa's Russian title is *Tretya Meshchanskaya,* or "Third Meshchanskaya Street." Playing on the Russian word *meshchanstvo,* or petit bourgeois, the film's title thus evokes both the sense of place and of social class crucial to its context.[2] The film tells the story of a woman, Ludmilla, whose life is defined by the tiny one-room apartment in which she spends her days. Her husband, Kolya, a construction supervisor, invites an old friend, a printer, to share their apartment. The friend, Volodya, has arrived recently in Moscow and cannot find a room because of the housing shortage. The husband is suddenly called out of town to work on a construction project. His departure is not unwelcome, for he is an arrogant chauvinist who treats his wife like a second-class citizen. Volodya, it seems, is different, for he makes no demands on Ludmilla and he treats her like an equal. Predictably, the two begin to sleep together during the husband's absence. When the husband returns and discovers what has happened, he leaves angrily. But he has no more luck in finding a room than did his friend, so the three settle down into a kind of extended marriage, with Ludmilla functioning as a wife to both men, regardless with which one she sleeps. Indeed, Volodya quickly assumes the same attitude toward Ludmilla that Kolya had, so that Ludmilla serves two masters instead of one. The ménage à trois, no matter how unconventional, changes nothing in the woman's position. When Ludmilla discovers that she is pregnant, the two men decide she should have an abortion, since neither welcomes the prospect of ambiguous paternity. Ludmilla goes to an abortion clinic. At the last minute she changes her mind, however. She leaves the two men to have and raise the child by herself.

Ludmilla is trapped within the confines of private life. While the two men move with ease from private to public space, Ludmilla has no such mobility. Thus *Bed and Sofa* presents the split between private and public life as a feature of everyday life in socialist society. That split emerges from the contradictions between traditional roles and radical change. Initially, Ludmilla's and Kolya's domestic life seems to be a function of his economic status as a supervisor. Scenes of him at work alternate between him supervising and others actually performing labor, suggesting that his arrogance at home— where he supervises and his wife performs the work—is an extension of his professional identity. The introduction of Volodya establishes him as a different type of man entirely. He is first seen in the film as his train approaches Moscow; he is associated with rapid movement and a more dynamic cinematic style than the couple. And perhaps most important, Volodya is a worker, not a supervisor. However, Volodya's emergence as a tyrant on the home front makes clear that sexual politics are not necessarily a simple reflection of class identity as defined by the workplace. Hence, the film refutes the notion that male members of the working class are necessarily more amenable to sexual equality than their petit-bourgeois counterparts. The private sphere, in *Bed and Sofa,* is directly connected to the public sphere, in the sense that the actions of the characters are thoroughly determined by material conditions (the housing shortage is at least in part responsible for the complicated triangle). More important, the film suggests that the interpersonal relationships of the characters are out of time with the economic changes in Soviet society, and not just a remnant of a past bound to wither away. Work and home in *Bed and Sofa* are separate in the sense that Kolya and Volodya work, while Ludmilla stays home and gets bored. Yet, Kolya is a creature of domesticity in his own right: when one of his co-workers asks him whether he will attend a political meeting that evening, he replies that he likes home better.

The relationship between the private and the public is depicted in a variety of ways. From the very outset, there is an opposition between motion and stasis. The film begins with several images of the city, followed by the one-room apartment where Ludmilla and Kolya are still asleep. The room is quite cluttered, and a series of shots reveals the still objects that are central to domestic routine: the sofa, a table and chairs, kitchen utensils. Sharp contrast with all of these still, motionless images is provided by a series of Volodya arriving by train in the city. The emphasis is on speed, with images of the track and the moving parts of the train shot from the train in motion. Volodya is designated as an active agent, as a man identified with a vital society in movement.

Images of the city and of Volodya's arrival continue to be intercut with images of the apartment, where Ludmilla and Kolya awake and perform their morning routines. A sense of harmony between the apartment and the city at large is suggested by a series of shots, beginning with the apartment's basement window. Through it can be seen a hose with which a worker washes the sidewalk. Images of Ludmilla washing at the sink, Kolya taking a shower, and their pet cat cleaning itself are followed by shots of a car being washed. Individual routines of everyday life are thus made part of a larger pattern. Already, however, there are some tensions introduced which will become more significant as the film develops. As the husband and wife wash, the man is depicted as infinitely more narcissistic and preoccupied with his body than is the woman. A straightforward, perfunctory image shows Ludmilla washing at the sink, whereas Kolya's shower occupies more screen time. And it is his body, rather than the woman's, that is displayed in close-up. The exterior world of the city is represented in two different ways: shots taken through the apartment window, and shots taken fully outdoors. The apartment window only allows a partial view of what goes on outside, since the basement vantage point offers a limited perspective, and the view is partially obscured by the curtains. In contrast, many of the outdoor shots emphasize depth and an overarching perspective on the city and its activities. Indeed, that perspective is soon identified with Kolya, who works on the roof of the Bolshoi Ballet, and takes his lunch break seated on a statue from which he commands a view of the entire city.[3]

As the film progresses, it becomes apparent that the harmony between the couple and the city suggested by the opening images of the film is more ideal than real. Husband and wife have radically different relationships to the outside world. The husband is as comfortable in public space as he is at home, while Ludmilla is enclosed and isolated within the domestic sphere, with the window as her only connection to the public sphere. In other words, Ludmilla's only relation to public space is through watching, through detached observation.

Volodya initially appears to be quite different from the arrogant, conceited Kolya. The speed, motion, and activity associated with his arrival are radically different from the characteristics of both Ludmilla's and Kolya's world. Volodya brings Ludmilla a radio and newspapers from the printing factory where he works, thus symbolically breaking down some barriers between home and work. These are means, for the woman, of connection, of involvement with the outside world from which she is so isolated. He even assists in performing domestic chores. Once the husband leaves, the friend's initial gestures are taken a step further. He accompanies Ludmilla outdoors and we see her for the first time in social space. He takes her on a plane ride, to which she reacts with childish glee. From the plane, we see the city, and a new perspective on social space, one even broader and more expansive than that of the statue from which, previously, Kolya gazed at the city. The airplane ride also recalls Volodya's arrival by train into the city, for the two of them are shot in a way quite similar to the earlier images of Volodya. She rides on a street car, and goes to the movies. With Volodya as mediator, Ludmilla finally takes a step toward mobility between home and city life. She still occupies the position of observer, but the limited perspective of her apartment window is replaced by broader scope and dynamic movement.

Given Volodya's attentiveness to Ludmilla, the sexual relationship between them seems quite inevitable. While Volodya's attentions seem to give Ludmilla a sense of fulfillment that has been lacking in her relationship with her husband, it is not clear the extent to which that fulfillment challenges, or reinforces, Ludmilla's petit-bourgeois identity. A very brief series of images, just prior to the husband's return, are quite suggestive in this regard. Ludmilla is in the apartment, seated in a rocking chair, mending one of Volodya's shirts. That she is daydreaming of Volodya is obvious, and shots of him at work are intercut with images of her. Volodya, as well as machinery at the factory, are seen in close-up, and the images recall the way in which he first appeared in the film, intercut with images of the moving parts of the train. The close-up of Volodya shows a pattern of light and shadow on his face, a pattern which recalls a similar pattern that was seen on Ludmilla's face when she first met Volodya (figs. 4.1 and 4.2). In that scene, she is changing clothes in the apartment and is startled when this stranger enters. She cowers next to a cane chair, through which the pattern of light and shadow falls on her face. This pattern, as it is seen on the faces of Ludmilla and Volodya in close-up, is an extremely condensed example of a device used in the film to suggest the distance between the apartment and the outside world. Early in the film, while husband and wife are engaged in their morning routine, a shot of the room shows the interplay of light and shadow projected from the figures walking along the street outside. As with the series of images depicting the morning ritual of washing, both inside and outside the apartment, it is not immediately clear whether the shadows signify the couple's participation in, or their separation from, the world outside. As the film progresses, however, the light and shadows come to be associated with Ludmilla, and with her isolation from the social world.

What, then, is the significance of the affinity between Ludmilla and Volodya suggested by this pattern of light and shadow, particularly since the pattern functions quite explicitly to signify *her* situation? To be sure, Volodya is crucial in his function as a mediator between Ludmilla and the world outside the apartment. It is one thing to be designated as a mediator, however, and quite another to be defined as Ludmilla's double. The visual similarity between the two close-ups is not the only indication of the strong affinity between Ludmilla and Volodya. For once Volodya sets up housekeeping on the sofa, pictures begin to appear on the wall next to it, making Volodya's individual space within the apartment something of a reflection of Ludmilla's vanity table, which is also surrounded by pictures.

It may well be that Volodya does function as a mirror, not just for Ludmilla, but for both her and Kolya. At the begin-

Fig. 4.1

Fig. 4.2

Fig.   4.3

ning of the film, Volodya is associated with a series of several images of the city, which have as a common theme water reflections. And the very first image of Volodya in the film, in the train, shows both him and his reflection in the train window (fig. 4.3). Volodya's identification with Ludmilla is, then, a kind of mirroring which in its initial stages, at least, has visible and positive effects on her. His reflective capacity suggests more of a possibility of a relationship between equals than is the case with Ludmilla and her husband. Less clear, however, are the effects that the identification has on him. The brief series of images showing Ludmilla sewing and Volodya at work suggest a common reverie. In the case of Ludmilla, the object of her thoughts is clear, particularly as she holds up Volodya's shirt and smiles. The close-ups of Volodya at work suggest, through the effects of montage, that she is indeed the object of his thoughts as well. However, this reciprocity is not firmly established. Montage establishes clearly that he is the object of her thoughts, but less clearly that she is the object of his. This ambiguity is reinforced by shots of the machinery in the factory, suggesting a parallel between the machinery and the shirt as the objects that define each character's work. But the terms are not really parallel, since Ludmilla has no association with the factory machinery, while the shirt virtually *is* Volodya.

Ludmilla's reverie is interrupted by the return of her husband. Later, when Volodya returns from work, Kolya hides, wanting to surprise his friend. When Volodya arrives, Kolya puts his hands over his friend's eyes. Volodya assumes, of course, that the hands belong to Ludmilla. He strokes Kolya's arm and kisses him enthusiastically. Kolya is none the wiser, and Ludmilla watches, amused. During an awkward dinner, Volodya finally tells Kolya about his and Ludmilla's relationship. The confession occurs while Ludmilla is away from the table. Despite the small size of the apartment, it is quickly divided into separate spheres. When the friend first moved in with the couple, Kolya put up a screen to divide the bed from the sofa. A more persistent division in the apartment is, however, represented by the curtain that separates the entryway and kitchen from the rest of the apartment, suggesting the sexual polarity that characterizes the domestic sphere. Ludmilla is located on the other side of the curtain when Volodya tells her husband what happened. A rather curious image depicts Ludmilla as she attempts to hear what is being said at the table. An extreme close-up of her is superimposed on the curtain, and her face seems to approach the camera (fig. 4.4). This kind of overt manipulation is very rare in the film, so it draws even more attention to Ludmilla's status as an alienated observer.

It is not the first time that Ludmilla has been represented as separate from the two men. When Kolya prepares to leave on his journey, he spends more time saying goodbye to his friend than to his wife. Cross-cutting depicts Ludmilla, packing her

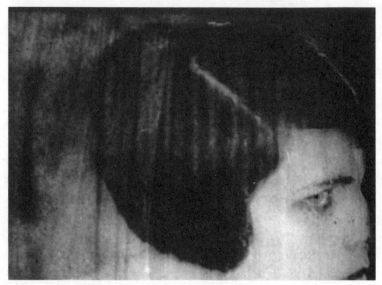

Fig.   4.4

husband's suitcase, and the two friends on the sofa discussing Kolya's departure. Ludmilla overhears her husband as he responds to Volodya's fears that people will talk if he stays in the apartment during the husband's absence. Kolya reassures his friend that Ludmilla is a devoted wife, and then makes a patronizing comment about a wife's subordination. Ludmilla angrily finishes packing for her husband, while he shows off his muscles to his friend. That Kolya and Volodya might be the real couple in *Bed and Sofa* is suggested here for the first time—that is, what Eve Kosofsky Sedgwick describes as male homosocial desire functions as a moving force of the film.[4] Ludmilla's absence during the confession of the affair takes the suggestion a step further, for it is as if the wife is only an object to be negotiated between the husband and the lover.[5]

Indeed, once the three agree to live together in the apartment, familiar patterns emerge. The two men spend more time with each other than with Ludmilla, who continues to occupy her place at the window. Volodya's transformation into a version of Kolya is demonstrated by a scene where he orders Ludmilla to make tea and then forbids her to leave the house. It is significant that this transformation does not occur until after the two men have become well established in their routines of tea, conversation, and games of checkers. In other words, whatever initial identification existed between Ludmilla and Volodya dissipates in the face of the much stronger identification between Volodya and Kolya. As Molly Haskell argues, the two men "have—in what is not an alteration but merely a multiplication of the usual domestic setup—succeeded in transforming the wife-mistress into a mother and in reverting quite happily to infancy."[6] And, as Beth Sullivan says, the "two men are together again—fraternity triumphs. Ludmilla is again the third party, ignored by both of them."[7] When Ludmilla begins sleeping with her husband again, it seems to have little impact on the threesome's living arrangements. Indeed, the dominant principle of this arrangement is to provide both men with the benefits of a home.

Room's film insists, then, that whether at the petit-bourgeois or the proletarian end of the spectrum, men have a major investment in maintaining traditional sexual relations. One of the benefits of traditional domestic arrangements is the affirmation, not only of male dominance, but of male fellowship as a principle governing the domestic as well as the social sphere. *Bed and Sofa* is certainly critical of how women are confined to domestic isolation, but its critique concerns not only how men relate to women, but also how men relate to each other. The fellowship between the two men is remarkably like what Kollontai described as characteristic of the earliest forms of social collectivity:

Love-friendship was the most suitable type of tie, since at that time the interests of the collective required the growth and accumulation of contacts not between the marriage pair but between fellow-members of the tribe, between the organisers and defenders of the tribe and state (that is to say, between the men of the tribe, of course; women at that time had no role to play in social life, and there was no talk of friendship among women). 'Friendship' was praised and considered far more important than love between man and wife.[8]

Kollontai assumed, of course, that women had become fully a part of social life in the Soviet Union at the time that this text was written (1923), but *Bed and Sofa* suggests that male friendship is nonetheless a persistent social and affective bond. And despite the fact that Kollontai is speaking of the distant past, in the passage cited, one suspects that the way in which the past is evoked is a function of what she witnessed in her own time.

Meanwhile, Ludmilla's pregnancy finally inspires her to leave the two men and go off on her own. She does go to an abortion clinic, but changes her mind just before her number is called. Ludmilla's decision to have the child rather than to have an abortion is not explained in any depth. Ludmilla is seated next to a window in the waiting room, thus adopting the familiar pose that characterizes her relationship to the world throughout the film. She opens the window to get some air, and sees a child playing with a doll. After an image of Ludmilla smiling, we see a close-up of a baby. A brief disruption in the waiting room occurs, and Ludmilla becomes distraught. Finally, she leaves. The nurse finds Ludmilla's number on her chair, and when she closes the window that Ludmilla left open, she sees two babies in the courtyard. Just what does lie beyond the window in the waiting room is not clear; one assumes that the close-up of a baby is a function of Ludmilla's imagination, but this does not explain why Ludmilla and the nurse see two different things. The point, however, is that, whatever actually lies on the other side of the window, it signifies only one thing for Ludmilla—the necessity of motherhood.[9] Throughout *Bed and Sofa,* the world on the other side of the window has been out of focus and abstract—partial objects and patterns of light and shadows. Suddenly, pregnancy gives her a different relationship to the window and to the world, with clearly defined, concrete babies replacing abstract forms. Yet, the awkwardness of the cuts, and the unclear relationship between what Ludmilla sees and what she imagines, suggests that motherhood may not be the obvious and self-evident alternative that the film seems to embrace.

When Ludmilla leaves at the end of the film, the two men remaining in the apartment may not be husband and wife, but they are most definitely creatures of domesticity. Thus, the relationship between private and public space is not determined absolutely by, nor reducible to, the opposition between male and female. The concluding images rhyme with the opening: Ludmilla leaves on a train, recalling Volodya's earlier arrival (figs. 4.5 and 4.6). She leaves the two men in a situation similar to that of the husband and wife at the beginning of the film. The airplane ride seemed to promise Ludmilla's release from the oppressive strictures of domestic life, but it was a false promise. Rather, it is motherhood that is the basis of Ludmilla's apparent autonomy.

The ideology of maternity thus presented in *Bed and Sofa* needs to be seen in relationship to the 1920s, when abortion was legalized but still regarded with deep suspicion, and when new legal definitions of sexual equality were not always reflected in day-to-day life. After Volodya and Ludmilla sleep together for the first time, he moves his things from the sofa to the bed, and they shake hands. Marriage and divorce may not have been simplified to the point of a simple handshake in the Soviet Union, but they required only a civil declaration by either party to be valid. While these new laws were meant to protect women's interests, particularly in giving the woman

Fig.   4.5

Fig.   4.6

the right to divorce, *Bed and Sofa* shows the other side of the coin, the so-called freedom to move from one "master" to another. To the obvious question of how women's legal and social autonomy is to be achieved, *Bed and Sofa* puts forth a rather pat answer: motherhood. Although the film does not explore the implications, one senses that Ludmilla, who has mothered both of the men in her life, is destined to be more fulfilled by mothering a child. In contemporary feminist terms, such a destiny seems to substitute one idealized view of woman (as mother) for another (as wife). The sudden appearance of motherhood as the answer to Ludmilla's problems in *Bed and Sofa* relies more on ideological simplicity than does the rest of the film. What is important to recognize, in evaluating the film in feminist terms, is the extent to which the issue of motherhood was problematic and contradictory, even for someone as committed to sexual equality and (eventually) feminism as Kollontai. After years of civil war and famine, an increased population was vital to the future of socialism. Abortion was legalized in the Soviet Union "on the grounds that it was a necessary evil."[10] Ludmilla hardly falls into the category of one for whom abortion was a necessary evil in Soviet terms; indeed, as Paul E. Burns writes, "Ludmilla's decision not to add to Moscow's abortion statistics positively conformed to the regime's desire to discourage this legal option."[11]

Kollontai wrote, "Soviet power realizes that the need for abortion will only disappear on the one hand when Russia has a broad and developed network of institutions protecting motherhood and providing social eduction, and on the other hand when women understand that *childbirth is a social obligation* . . ."[12] The missing link in Kollontai's formulation is who, or what, decides just what constitutes social obligations. However, seen from the perspective of social obligation, Ludmilla's decision to have the child is the decisive step toward her own socialization. At the conclusion of the film, Ludmilla's claim to autonomy is accentuated by the photograph of herself that she takes with her, leaving a blank frame on the wall. Similarly, she leaves a note for the two men, telling them that neither is worthy to be the child's father. But the resolution of the film is even more convincing as a sign of Ludmilla's acceptance of her social obligation. Of course, the question of why autonomy and social obligation have to be in opposition to each other could be asked. They do not, but the point is that this tension—between self-realization and social obligation—is one the film cannot resolve.

The specifically narrative implications of sexual politics, and of the connection between the private and the public in *Bed and Sofa,* are better revealed perhaps, by looking at the film in relationship to Kollontai's fictional work. In 1923, she published the novella "Vasilisa Malygina." This story is about a man and wife who, after the revolution, work in separate cities. Both continue to be active revolutionaries, although the husband, partly because of his new job as a factory manager, becomes increasingly conservative in his views. Under political attack, he wires Vasilisa to come to him. The background of their relationship is told in flashback during Vasilisa's train ride. The relationship is disturbed by the increasing political differences between the two, and by the fact that he has a mistress. They eventually separate and Vasilisa returns to her former job.

There are many similarities between Kollontai's novella and *Bed and Sofa.* While Vasilisa, unlike Ludmilla, is a committed revolutionary, both women characters resist the isolation of domesticity. Vasilisa does so consciously, and Ludmilla unconsciously, until the shock of recognition in the abortion clinic. In both stories, the final triumph, of sorts, is pregnancy. When Vasilisa discovers she is pregnant shortly after returning to her job, she, like Ludmilla (although for different reasons) rejects the possibility of abortion. Instead her pregnancy motivates her to move forward with her ideas for a communal house where the child—"a communist baby!"—will be raised collectively.

Personal life is experienced through the customs and habits of domesticity in both "Vasilisa Malygina" and *Bed and Sofa*. It is especially interesting to note that in the short story, Vladimir, the husband, is more attached to a traditional form of domestic life than is his wife. Whereas Vasilisa lives in a single, poorly furnished room, Vladimir owns a luxuriously furnished apartment over which he constantly fusses, insisting that the curtains be kept closed so that the furniture will not fade. It is Vasilisa who symbolically violates the sanctity of Vladimir's shrine of privatized space, when she invites some labor leaders into the house to discuss political strategy. Her husband is outraged. Vasilisa's own relationship to private life is represented in the novel by the frequent evocation of the communal house, a project violently opposed and drastically misunderstood by her co-workers and her husband.

. . . Vladimir was always having fantasies about his new job and how they'd set up house and arrange their domestic affairs, all of which Vasya found very tedious. What was the point of having your own house? Where was the pleasure in it? It would have been quite different if they'd been establishing a communal house, but Vladimir disagreed violently with her on this and attacked her "conservatism."[13]

Kollontai's novella goes considerably further than *Bed and Sofa* in developing the ideological implications of the conflict over different modes of personal life. Also, Vladimir's attachment to a refined, conventionally bourgeois private sphere is a function of his own socioeconomic status; he is clearly a product of NEP. In *Bed and Sofa*, there is certainly a tension concerning private life, but it never is articulated in the sophisticated and antagonistic political terms of Kollontai's short story, and Ludmilla is far from being the political activist that Vasilisa is. Nonetheless, the two texts share an important trait, for they are both attempts to understand and explore the historical conditions that shape the interrelationship of private and public life, and the relationships between men and women.

Where the two works are less convincing, however, is in their representation of pregnancy as a simultaneous narrative resolution and a form of emancipation. *Mother* comes immediately to mind. One wonders if the mother-child relationship in these two works is, as in Pudovkin's film, symbolic of a natural destiny fulfilled through political activity. However, neither *Bed and Sofa* nor "Vasilisa Malygina" recounts a conversion from apolitical to political, which is the span of motherhood as represented in Pudovkin's film. At the root of *Mother* is a notion of extreme dialectical change, and the change from conservative to socialist automatically makes motherhood a more fulfilling experience. In *Bed and Sofa,* there is no indication of Ludmilla's being politically active, and Vasilisa is already a committed revolutionary. Thus, motherhood does not carry quite the amount of extensive metaphoric burden that it does in *Mother.*

Yet, like Pudovkin's film, motherhood in *Bed and Sofa* and "Vasilisa Malygina" is the means by which individual and social selves are consolidated. The birth of her child marks Vasilisa's recommitment, not to communist principles—there was never, in her conflicts with her husband, any question of abandoning them in the first place—but to the possibility of personal life being lived in political terms. Hence, Vasilisa returns to the project of a communal house, temporarily abandoned during her problems with her husband. Ludmilla's departure at the conclusion of *Bed and Sofa* places her decision to have the child by herself—regardless of who the father is—in the space between home and social world. The final image

of Ludmilla in the film shows her inside the train compartment, looking eagerly out of the window: the image is like
many others of her in the film, but she is no longer trapped
within the four walls of her domestic life.

Certainly, there are suggestions of a female destiny finally
being fulfilled in these two works. But, whereas motherhood
functions as a mediation between domestic and social space
for both women characters, the process is quite different than
in *Mother.* In *Mother,* there is little exploration of contradiction.
Revolutionary commitment becomes a simple logical movement, with no detours or hesitations. Hence, *Mother* represses
any further appearance of domesticity after the mother's
change of consciousness. Kollontai's novella is an effort to
expose contradiction, and it is an appropriate grid through
which to read *Bed and Sofa,* a similar attempt to work through
the various facets of domestic life. Even if a sense of natural
female destiny does emerge, there is no mystified realm of
Nature to function as a grand metaphor of socialist consciousness. Kolya and Volodya do not quite know what to do
with themselves when a woman upsets the traditional balance
between personal and social existence, and when their own
mobility between the two spheres suddenly is posed as problematic. The men in *Bed and Sofa* are left to deal with the
institution of domesticity, and the very fact that they, too, are
fast becoming passive homebodies suggests that the contours
of private and public life are as historically determined as the
relationship between male and female identities.

5. *Fragment of an Empire* and the Woman in the Window

IN VIRTUALLY all Soviet films of the 1920s, the examination of history is a key component. Hence, many of the narrative strategies of these films center on the representation of the past, and more important, on the connection between the pre-revolutionary past, as symbolized by the disarray of the workers' movement in *Strike*, or the nascent revolutionary consciousness of the mother in *Mother*, and the present. Even *Bed and Sofa*, a film much more connected to the contemporary state of Russian socialism, creates a perspective on the present by putting into question forms of behavior and interaction more representative of, and more appropriate to, the pre-revolutionary past. A crucial component of the relationship between past and present is spectatorship, both in terms of how the films assume certain responses, and of how figures of vision and observation are set up within the films, whether through individual characters or through other cinematic and narrative strategies. Images of displaced vision in *Strike*, the cycles of nature in *Mother*, and the isolation of a woman within domestic space in *Bed and Sofa*, suggest diverse vantage points on historical change. Like *Strike* and *Mother*, Ermler's 1929 film, *Fragment of an Empire*, explores the relationship between the pre-revolutionary past and the present. However, this film

offers a rather unique narrative formulation of that relationship. The central character in the film is a man, portrayed
by the remarkable actor Fyodor Nikitin, who lost his memory
during World War I, only to regain it ten years after the revolution. While the notion is hardly original, this story of an
outsider's confused and bewildered responses to a society that
has changed drastically during his amnesia, raises some interesting questions concerning narrative agency and authority.
In this film, narrational perspective is more closely aligned
with a single character than in the other films considered thus
far. Needless to say, however confused the man is initially by
the changes that have occurred during his amnesia, he becomes an enthusiastic convert to the spirit of revolutionary
change. The narrative thus serves a precise ideological end. At
the same time, even though the over-arching perspective of the
film is so closely identified with a single character, there is a
space in the film, a gap, that problematizes the secure fit
between past and present and all the other oppositions that
the film wishes to reconcile through the central character's
restoration of memory. Although it does so in quite different
ways from the films previously examined, *Fragment of an
Empire* nonetheless turns centrally on a similar figure—that of
the woman. In *Fragment of an Empire,* the figure of woman
functions more profoundly than in the other films to complicate the narrative trajectory and framework of the film. What
this figure of woman demonstrates, then, is the difficulty of
articulating a new narrative and cinematic consciousness for
socialism. That difficulty arises precisely at the point where
socialist narrative consciousness requires some of the same
functions of the figure of woman as the presumably outmoded and reactionary forms of the past do.

Fragment of an Empire traces the steps necessary to restore the
memory of Fillimonov, the amnesia victim. The first glimpses
of a recognizable past occur at a train station early in the film.

Fillimonov sees a woman's face in a train compartment and is inexplicably captivated. He returns home, and through a complex combination of images, everyday objects, and a sewing machine, he gradually begins to retrieve his past. The woman in question was his wife. Fillimonov goes to Leningrad with his restored identity, only to be completely baffled by the social changes that have taken place. He begins to adjust to new living conditions, and he becomes a factory worker. At the conclusion of the film he finds his former wife, whose briefly perceived face began the process by which his memory was restored. She has become a privileged member of Soviet society, and is married to a moronic cultural worker. Although she is tempted to leave him to return to her former husband, she does not.

Fillimonov's memory is restored in several distinct stages. The film opens with a prologue of sorts, at a train station during the Civil War. The bodies of dead soldiers have been removed from trains, and Fillimonov wanders among the bodies and removes the boots from them. He sees that a young soldier is still alive. The soldier is lying on the ground in a barn, and he crawls toward a mother dog nursing her pups. Several soldiers enter the barn and one of them pulls out a gun and shoots, not the soldier, but the dog. Fillimonov immediately begins to care for the young soldier, and his function as a nurturing figure is accentuated by the cutting between him, the young soldier, and the slain mother dog whose pups still nurse at her side. From the outset, then, Fillimonov is identified as being somewhat removed from the realm of masculine endeavor. Not only is he not on either side, as far as the lines between soldiers are drawn, but his association with the mother dog strongly suggests that he fulfills a nurturing, female role.

The prologue ends with an image of the young soldier in Fillimonov's arms, with Fillimonov stroking his head. Suddenly, the focus shifts, as the temporal register of the film moves forward. If the prologue establishes Fillimonov as a figure of nurturance and care-taking, the shots that follow suggest that he is a child. Fillimonov is scrubbing floors inside his house, and he pauses to play gleefully with a paper boat. Children appear at the window and take him with them to the train station. Here again, Fillimonov bears witness as a kind of helpless bystander. He dimly recognizes the woman he sees in a train compartment, and her shocked reaction affirms the recognition. However, he cannot fit the image into his own frame of reference. Hence, from the outset, *Fragment of an Empire* represents two kinds of past tense. First, there is the past tense of the war, represented as a fragment with no visible connection to the present tense. Second, there is the past tense of a single image of a woman, the significance of which is unclear to the man. These two forms correspond to the difference between the public sphere—the war, the official realm of history—and the private sphere, a relationship between a man and a woman. Within each of these realms, there is a strong sense of identification conveyed by an exchange of glances, first between the young soldier and Fillimonov, and later between Fillimonov and the woman at the train station.

Images of wartime and a woman are juxtaposed, and it is after the encounter with the woman's face at the train station that the process of restoration of memory begins. Images surge forth in rapid succession, and the man, seated at the sewing machine, begins the process of stitching together, literally and metaphorically, the pieces of his past and present selves. This scene, a stunning example of the use of cinematic montage, is the narrative center of the film. It functions as a visual and narrative matrix; its components are reactivated throughout the film, forming various configurations of the relation between past and present.

Fig.   5.1

Fig.   5.2

Fig.   5.3

Fig.   5.4

   The sequence begins with the relatively simple exchange of looks between the man on the platform and the woman looking out of the train compartment window. Fillimonov is bewildered, and the woman is shocked; the intensity of the recognition is conveyed by the increasingly close angle of the shots of each character (figs. 5.1–5.4). She moves away from the window as the train bell begins to ring. Fillimonov, confused, speaks to the train conductor and then turns to the train. She has disappeared, and he sees only other faces, or empty windows. Outside of the train window where he had seen her, however, he picks up a cigarette box that had been thrown from within the compartment.

   The exchange of looks between the man and the woman is represented in shot-reverse shot. In the prologue of the film, there was a similar exchange of looks between the officer and the dog, the officer and the young soldier, and between the young soldier and Fillimonov. The young soldier faces screen left, while the officer and Fillimonov, in turn, face screen right. When the man's and woman's eyes first meet on the train platform, the man occupies the same position as the young soldier in the previous sequence. She, however, occupies the positions of both the officer and Fillimonov. The repetition of shot-reverse shot thus functions to establish an equation between the young soldier and Fillimonov—both have been victimized, and both are in need of care. The reversal of roles is not complete, however, for the woman here does not function as caretaker. Rather, her function is first and foremost that of image—an image located in an ambivalent space between the brutal officer and the man who offers his help.

After the man returns home with the cigarette box, the piecing together of images, the restoration of memory, begins. This process occurs in four basic stages. First, the association between two concrete objects has a sparklike effect. The man picks up a toy bell from a table and rings it. In rapid succession, the toy bell, the bell ringing at the train station, and the cigarette box, which the man clutches, move across the screen. An alternating series of images moves at breakneck speed: various shots of the woman, all in close-up—some identical to those seen previously and some from other contexts, including one where she wears a wedding dress—and images of a rapidly moving train. The alternating series closes with a shot of Fillimonov, still clutching the box. He opens it gingerly to peek inside, as if it were a kind of Pandora's box of his own past.

During this first stage, then, the man appears to have as little control over the sudden surge of images as he would over the rapidly moving train depicted in the sequence. In the second stage, the man takes a more active role in connecting the images, so that the emphasis is on the process rather than on the images perceived in isolation. An image of the woman appears, out of focus, as if it is receding from the man's consciousness. He begins to turn the handle of the sewing machine on the table in front of him. Again, there is an alternating series of two image tracks. Close-ups of Fillimonov's face alternate with parts of the sewing machine in rapid movement. The alternating structure is quite similar to that of the previous stage, with images of the man's face substituting for the woman's, and images of the sewing machine taking the place of the train. The rapid pace of the cutting is dizzying, even more so than in the previous stage. It continues, and the alternating pattern expands considerably to include images of the train whistle, the woman's face, and the officer from the prologue of the film. Then the pace slows down, and Fillimonov sees in other everyday objects surrounding him connections to the images that just surged forth. As he looks attentively at a spool of thread rolling across the table, the image dissolves to a tank on a battleground. As he moves to pick up the spool, his attention is caught by an iron cross around his neck. He holds the cross, then bites it; and, as if on cue, more images from his past appear on screen, beginning with images of an assortment of religious crosses.

In the first stage of memory production, Fillimonov's own past is mediated by what just preceded, the scene of recognition at the train station. Both the cigarette box and the bell, crucial elements in the sudden burst of images from the past, are associated with that scene. The man's ability to connect them to the immediate past is the simplest form of association. In the second stage, however, memory becomes a more active process. Thus, the spool and the iron cross represent more complex connections to Fillimonov's past than the cigarette box or the bell. This is, in part, because the past in question is the more distant past of the man, rather than the immediate past of the film. The movement of the spool across the table suggests the movement of a tank because a more complex metaphoric process takes the place of the simple association of the previous stage. Since it has an immediate symbolic function within the context of war, the iron cross is more like the cigarette box and the bell. However, the process of association concerning the cross is more complex than what has been seen thus far; a detour is required, through the religious symbolism of the cross, before an actual war scene is reconstructed.

The third stage of memory production begins when the images evoked are combined to form a more complex whole, a story. The story told is abstract and dreamlike. Fillimonov sees himself on a battlefield, confronting his mirror reflection, another soldier, his double. Each is spurred on by superior officers screaming from the sidelines (the same man in each case). The two men—that is, Fillimonov and his double—refuse to fire. One of them is, however, felled by a bomb explosion. While this episode might function as the explanation of Fillimonov's amnesia, even more important is the fact that the capacity to imagine a story is the first action that symbolizes the restoration of his memory. The representation of this episode requires that connections be made between different elements of Fillimonov's past, as well as between the past and the present. Enormously suggestive in this regard is the final image of the story. The man lies in the mud after the bomb has exploded, and the next image shows Fillimonov in the present, lying in exactly the same position (figs. 5.5 and 5.6). Fillimonov now sees himself as a creature of both the past and the present, as the use of the mirror double rather obviously suggests. He functions as both storyteller and as subject, and not just as a helpless, passive observer of images drawn randomly from his own past.

The fourth stage of memory production begins when the woman for whom Fillimonov works returns to the house. He

Fig. 5.5

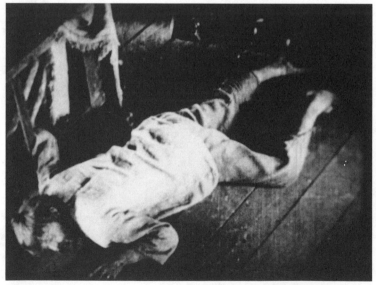

Fig. 5.6

describes to her what has just taken place. The reporting of his experience to another observer is yet another form of story telling, one which requires more conscious effort than the preceding dreamlike story. When Fillimonov explains what has happened, the accompanying images on the screen are the same as those in the first stage of the reconstruction of his memory—the woman (now clearly identified as his former wife) and the rapidly moving train. But in the present context, the images have another frame of reference. Previously, these images were the means by which the man had access to his past. Yet, even in his rediscovery of the past, those original images still remain a mystery to him. Unlike the images of war, which have been explained and put in their proper place, the images of the woman and the incident at the train station still exist as enigmas in the present. A description of those images, then, initiates the quest for a discovery of their significance.

In this reconstruction the most important single object is the sewing machine. The rapid succession of images is synchronized to the rapid movements of the machine. If it is quite obvious that Fillimonov sews together the bits and pieces of his past, the metaphor of sewing and stitching also raises some less obvious questions. The process of memory, which is presented in the film as the form of consciousness itself, is analogous to work. However, one wonders why it is stereotypically *female* work that provides the quintessential metaphor here. As I've already suggested, Fillimonov is defined from the outset as an outsider in the world of men, or at the very least, in the stereotypically masculine pursuits of war. In relationship to an image of woman, he is incapable of assuming a position of authority or desire. The woman represents, even after the cathartic experience with the sewing machine, a mystery to be solved. *Fragment of an Empire* articulates a view of socialist change as eminently desirable when seen through the eyes of a man who makes the transition abruptly and traumatically,

but ultimately unscathed and all the happier and more fulfilled for it. At the same time, the film attempts to articulate a
psychic trajectory for the changes brought on by socialism.
For Fillimonov's quest is that of a child who becomes an
adult. In this sense, the film is suggestive of *Mother,* where the
relationship between mother and son equates psychic and
emotional maturity with political consciousness. Like *Mother,*
Fragment of an Empire attempts to fuse socialization into the
socialist public sphere with the emergence of individual identity. But the oedipal trajectory of *Mother* relies on a more pre-
dictable and conventional narrative structure. True, the process traced in *Fragment of an Empire* is uniquely male-centered
and presupposes socialist fellowship as a fellowship of men.
But there is another dimension to the process. In attempting
to articulate the psychic basis of socialist culture, the film
raises questions concerning loss and identification which it is
unable to answer. *Fragment of an Empire* is a rather unique film
in this sense, for its vision of the desirability of socialist change
coexists with a vision of the inevitability of loss implicit in any
process of maturation, socialist or otherwise.

Fillimonov's restoration of memory involves a measure of
control and mastery. The special function of montage in this
venture becomes particularly apparent; there are few other
instances in *Fragment of an Empire* when rapid montage, such as
that used in the memory-production sequence, occurs.
Another takes place after Fillimonov's arrival in Leningrad,
where he becomes considerably perplexed by socialist change.
He demands to know "who is master here?" Factory workers
explain to him that the Soviet Union is now a workers' state,
then a rapid montage sequence depicts various aspects of
labor. Thus, the most stunning and self-conscious demonstrations of montage serve to illustrate the processes of individual
and social mastery simultaneously.

Perhaps the self-referential function of the sewing machine

is most obvious. The restoration of Fillimonov's memory is a figure of the cinema itself, for what else is montage than the piecing together of images to create context and meaning? The metaphor condenses labor and cinematic vision, thus cinema is defined as a process of production. Indeed, the memory that *Fragment of an Empire* describes is also the memory that it produces, that is, the fusion of images to create new and complex wholes.

The process whereby Fillimonov is healed functions, of course, as a metaphor for the process of rebirth and social change. Hence, the integration of private and public selves is as key to Fillimonov's recovery as it is to the vision of socialist change produced in the film. However, the spheres of private and public life, represented by images of woman and wartime, do not have equal significance. If the man's relationship to his military past is solved relatively quickly and efficiently in the film, his relationship to his personal past, and to the image of woman that functions to evoke it, is considerably more problematic. After Fillimonov's identity has been stitched together successfully, he continues to carry with him the iron cross, a powerful symbol not only of the past that has been restored to him, but of the importance of symbolic relationships in that process of restoration. The image of his former wife, however, has no corresponding symbol in Fillimonov's consciousness. Rather, the image of the woman is a more diffuse presence in the film. It is not contained by a single symbolic object, but is evoked by a variety of objects throughout the film. Indeed, only at the end does Fillimonov encounter this precise image again. It is his memory of the woman that marks the film's departure from a strict and narrow identification with the perspective of Fillimonov. For even while she seems to recede from his consciousness, the film reminds us— literally, by showing her present whereabouts, and implicitly, by representing women in problematic ways—that she represents another mystery to be solved, a significant piece of the puzzle to be fit into place.

When Fillimonov arrives in Leningrad with his new capacity to remember and his newly acquired sense of identity, the restoration of memory moves into another stage, one shaped by the collision between a society that has experienced a decade of radical social change, and an individual who has been oblivious to that change. Fillimonov's memory is out of time with the social changes that have taken place. He is puzzled by a statue of Lenin and shocked by women's exposed legs on a bus. His responses are childlike, reinforcing Fillimonov's role as a child being reborn into a new social order. That it should be an image of a woman's body that evokes a sense of embarrassment suggests, of course, that the "woman question" is one which remains to be confronted by Fillimonov.

When he goes to visit his former employer, Fillimonov is dismayed to find that he and his wife live in a pitiful state—poor, disheveled, and just as out of time, albeit for different reasons, with present-day life as Fillimonov himself. Fillimonov's memory functions metaphorically in relation to several oppositions within Soviet culture because the relationship of outsider and insider is defined and shaped not just by the extreme situation of one such as Fillimonov, but also by the situations of those such as his former employer and his wife, who occupy an alienated position within Soviet life. The encounter with Fillimonov becomes, for them, a memory of how things used to be. Two conflicting perspectives define the representation of the couple. Fillimonov perceives them only as victims of inexplicable change. Yet, they are, at the same time, presented to the implicit spectator of *Fragment of an Empire* as stereotypical, self-righteous capitalists.

Fillimonov's arrival in Leningrad marks an increasing separation between his perspective and a perspective more defined by what was, in 1929, a shared set of iconographic conventions. If, in the first part of *Fragment of an Empire,* the film's perspective is defined almost exclusively with Fillimonov's consciousness, his move to Leningrad initiates another kind of narration, whereby an individual and a social point of view constantly collide. The film taps some easily recognizable elements of socialist mythology: stereotyped capitalists, rugged workers, effete bureaucrats, efficient factories and cooperatives. This is not to say that the film merely presents these images in a self-congratulatory way; rather, the collision between two points of view creates the possibility for some rather pointed social criticism. [1]

As Fillimonov attempts to adjust to the new conditions surrounding him, images from the earlier sequences of the film reappear in various ways. Fillimonov's former employer gives him a note to take to a factory center. Inside the center, he sees a room where people are eating at large tables. A man is speaking at a microphone. In yet another demonstration of how naïve and unsocialized Fillimonov is, he marches to the podium to show the speaker his letter. Predictably, he is rebuffed. However, other workers take charge of Fillimonov and show him around. Among the workers is a familiar face: the young soldier from the prologue. He recognizes Fillimonov as the man who was responsible for nursing him back to health. Hence, within the factory center, the film recaptures its own beginning, as the man's past becomes woven into a social fabric. More important, the film suggests that a reversal will occur now; that the young man, who is a representative of the new social order, will return to Fillimonov the same nurturance and care that he had administered to the young man in the past. The reversal suggests, of course, that what Fillimonov had offered the young soldier now exists in broader, social terms.

The former wife of Fillimonov also reappears, although she is shown to the viewer long before she is shown to Fillimonov.

In yet another extraordinary coincidence, the speaker who did not appreciate being interrupted by Fillimonov is the woman's present husband. The couple is introduced in a scene just before Fillimonov's arrival at the factory center. The woman brushes her husband's suit while he eats breakfast. She is, thus, also identified as a caretaker, although her gestures seem superfluous in the present context, in contrast to those of her former husband in the life-and-death context of war. Once Fillimonov's memory has been restored, the film develops a more complex structure of point of view. As they appear, images of the former wife are connected to other oppositions, and not just the opposition between past and present in relation to which they were first introduced. If her caretaking activities are contrasted with those of Fillimonov in the past, the domestic life which she and her husband share is contrasted sharply with the collective spirit at the factory center in the present. And, perhaps most significantly, the woman remains, for Fillimonov, an unconscious presence.

Various objects function as instruments in Fillimonov's piecing-together of his past: the cigarette package discarded from the woman's train compartment; the sewing machine; the spool's movement across the table which evokes the image of a tank's movement; and the iron cross which suddenly is endowed with its own sort of history. As Fillimonov responds and adjusts to the new society that he sees, all of these elements reappear in different contexts. The comradeship abstractly expressed between the two soldiers (his two selves) in his memory is refined and expanded in the relationships between Fillimonov and his co-workers at the factory. The military generals' authority is mirrored in his former employer. The sewing machine, the central instrument in reactivating his past, is mirrored by the machines which provide the basis for his reintegration into Soviet society. In what is surely the most overt symbolic gesture of Fillimonov's ability to put his

newly discovered past behind him, he gives away his iron cross
to a theatrical group. The cross thus becomes a relic providing
a no-longer necessary contact with the past. Once he becomes
a part of production and of a social collective, the film suggests, elements of Fillimonov's own past are both made sense
of and qualitatively transformed. In other words, the man's
individual past is first evoked in an incomplete way, and only
becomes part of a whole once he has a place, a nascent identity, within a collective.

The process of integrating elements of Fillimonov's past
into the present appears to be total and all-encompassing.
However, virtually every sign associated with women is ren-
dered in an ambiguous way. When workers at the factory
center explain factory machinery to him, a woman inspector
appears. Later she introduces herself to Fillimonov and shakes
his hand. Fillimonov seems to be stunned, and later sees
workers making fun of how he responded to the woman in
such a stiff, formal way. This leads to the stunning montage
sequence prompted by Fillimonov's question, "who is master
here?" In a brief sequence clearly designed to represent what is
going on in Fillimonov's mind, shots of machines in the factory are followed by Fillimonov's former boss fainting, as he
did during Fillimonov's visit. Hence, it would appear that
Fillimonov's question concerns ownership of the factory. Yet,
at the same time, the question is prompted by his confusion
that a woman should occupy a position of authority. If the
workers at the factory provide satisfying answers concerning
the social changes that have occurred since the revolution, the
issue of gender is left unaddressed. And while the film does
show women workers at the factory, the community of which
Fillimonov becomes a part is predominantly a fellowship of
men. The images which convey most strikingly Fillimonov's
integration into this community portray uniquely male envi-
ronments, such as the collective showers and the barracks.

One reviewer put it quite succinctly; after Fillimonov's arrival in the city, "[t]he rest of the film concerns the fitting in of the peasant with a life of showers and razors."[2]

Yet, the film constantly reminds us of the nagging woman question, if not in purely socialist terms then at least in terms of the unresolved areas of Fillimonov's past. Fillimonov is as embarrassed by women's legs displayed in the bus as he is taken aback by women in roles of authority at the factory. His encounter with his former boss involves witnessing the decay, not only of the man's social position, but also of his domestic life, and the presence of the boss's wife is yet another reminder of Fillimonov's own past. The film seems to avoid addressing a feminist issue by stressing that workers are in control of their destinies, making gender at best a category of secondary importance. However, this is a secondary status that the film cannot and does not sustain.

When he at last goes to visit his former wife, the final stage of Fillimonov's memory restoration occurs. Her address has been obtained for him by the former soldier. Fillimonov's only image of her has been against a blank background, whereas when he enters her apartment, he sees her surrounded by numerous objects depicting a cluttered existence. That the scene is meant to convey closure is suggested by the appearance of a cigarette box, in close-up, similar to the box which was Fillimonov's only tangible link to the fleeting image of his wife at the train station. The first scenes at the factory center established the young soldier seen in the prologue within the present tense of the film, and this scene performs a parallel function with respect to the woman. The climactic nature of this sequence also is assured by the reappearance, for the first time, of some images from the early sequence in the film when Fillimonov, with the assistance of the sewing machine, pieced together his past.

The woman's present husband is just as pompous and

overbearing as he appeared to be at the factory center. Before Fillimonov's arrival, the husband complains to his wife that she has put too much salt in the soup. When Fillimonov arrives, he leaps in joy and showers his former wife with kisses. If Fillimonov appeared to be a child at the beginning of the film, here he seems to have reached adolescence. A quarrel ensues between Fillimonov's former wife and her husband, and the husband pushes her. As Fillimonov prepares to hit the husband, there is a brief, fast montage sequence in which the husband's face is intercut with images of the officer who shot the dog in the prologue, of another officer from the dream-like remembrance that Fillimonov had of the war; and of a worker, in the present tense of the film, whom Fillimonov found drinking on the job. These images give Fillimonov pause. They suggest, of course, an affinity between the husband, the outmoded authority figures of a military past, and the alienated figure of the revolutionary present. These images also function as a rapid summary of the past. Fillimonov looks around the room and, for the first time, it is apparent that he is capable not only of putting images together, but of reading them critically. The apartment is shown in a series of shots as fragmented as the original representation of his own relationship to the past. Virtually every one depicts a self-contained object: a pamphlet covered with soup, a still life, a complete set of Lenin's works.[3] Finally, there is an image of the woman, much like the images seen previously, although now she is defined within what the viewer might assume to be *her* context, rather than Fillimonov's memory of her. Leyda says of the conclusion to the film that Fillimonov must "face the most difficult problem of all—to watch his wife struggle unsuccessfully with an ancient set of conventions."[4] While I would not disagree that the domestic and social conventions seen in *Fragment of an Empire* are ancient, it is questionable to what extent there is any kind of struggle waged. The woman has existed as nothing more than a series of projections, whether they be Fillimonov's, her present husband's, or those of the film itself.

Although the pace is much slower, the flow of images in the conclusion is evocative of the memory sequence. The resemblance suggests the resolution of past and present tense, as well as the ability to see the past as both in the present and removed from it. Ideologically, the film wants to suggest that once Fillimonov has become a productive member of socialist society, whatever questions remain in his own personal past will be cast in a different, less perplexing light.[5] Just before Fillimonov goes to his wife's apartment, he is engaged in a lively political discussion with other factory workers in a communal dormitory. The active, dynamic atmosphere of the dormitory contrasts with the couple's apartment. The man and wife have little to say to each other, and her submission to him is "ancient" indeed. Thus the tension between past and present in the film connects to another opposition between two forms of personal life—one lived collectively, the other more traditionally, hierarchically, and individually. The relationship between the past and the present changes from temporal to spatial dimensions; the outmoded forms of a reactionary past are shown to coexist, in Soviet society, with the revolutionary fellowship of the dormitory. This contrast is strikingly conveyed by the shift from one space to another.

While the film seems to affirm that Fillimonov's process of transformation places him in absolute contrast to his former wife and her present husband, such a neatly defined opposition would suggest both the irrevocable distance between bourgeois and socialist conceptions of everyday life, and the capacity of socialist culture to integrate what remains as conflict and alienation in a capitalist society. However, this resolution to *Fragment of an Empire* is not presented unambiguously. A small textual detail that marks the transition from

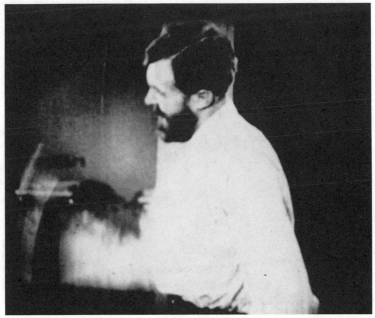

Fig.   5.7

the dormitory, where Fillimonov talks enthusiastically with
his new-found comrades, to the apartment shared by the couple, is enormously significant in this regard. At the conclusion
of the first scene, Fillimonov is depicted in profile from the
waist it up, facing screen left while his right hand bobs up and
down, vigorously affirming a political point. The next shot
depicts the woman's present husband, in their apartment,
standing in the same position as Fillimonov in the previous
shot, his hand in an identical movement (figs. 5.7 and 5.8).
The cut recalls the earlier, climactic scene in which Fillimonov's body is seen stretched out on the ground during
the dreamlike battlefield memory, followed by a scene in the
present in which he occupies exactly the same position on the
floor of his house. In that earlier sequence, the repetition suggests the strong imprint of the past, now becoming an integral

Fig.   5.8

part of Fillimonov's present. What, then, of the similar repetition at the conclusion of the film? It is tempting to argue that, here, the match between the two images suggests the absolute difference between the two men. If this is indeed the case, it is a difference too much marked by similarity to be convincing. While it might be interesting to argue that the hero of *Fragment of an Empire* is quickly turning into an obnoxious bureaucrat, I would suggest, rather, that this detail suggests a problem that the film really cannot resolve. At this moment in the film, there is the possibility of a full recapture of the past for Fillimonov. It is not surprising that in a film so preoccupied with loss, with the restoration of memory as a painful and painstaking process, there should be no absolute restoration of memory possible. Indeed, this feature of *Fragment of an Empire* makes it impossible to classify the film as purely and simply a vehicle for socialist ideology. But if it is, therefore, impossible to capture that image of woman and to fix it in the present, what is the relationship of Fillimonov to that image? The detail I have described suggests, however sketchily, that whatever the differences between the moronic present husband and Fillimonov, they assume a relationship to discourse that requires the containment of woman as an enticing but ultimately unattainable object.

Woman signifies, in Ermler's film, the private and the domestic, as well as a part of the past that remains unattainable. Of all the elements that appear in the original memory sequence, the image of the former wife reappears in the most static way. Briefly perceived at the train station, she is one of many images in Fillimonov's past; and perceived again by him at the end of the film, she functions in much the same way. All the other elements of the man's past—the military, figures of authority, machinery—have been qualitatively redefined in a passage from past to present and from individual to social. However, the woman is as rigidly locked into the claustrophobic private space of her domestic life with her husband as she was locked into Fillimonov's past. *Fragment of an Empire* makes an absolute association between woman as image, and woman as a creature of private space. The wife is initially perceived in the film as an image, framed by the train window, and then as a series of multiple images, sewn together as pieces of filmstrip through the movements of the sewing machine. If the woman is first and foremost an image, she remains an image because she never leaves the immediate space of private life. It could be argued, of course, that this is precisely the point of Ermler's film—that no true emancipation of woman from her status as image is possible as long as she remains defined by traditional domestic life. I do not see the film as engaging in such a critique, but this is not necessarily because I am cynical about the possibilities of male socialist filmmakers engaging with issues of sexual equality and gender difference. In *this* film, the issues of loss, rebirth and regeneration so intimately tied to Fillimonov's amnesia and subsequent recovery are posed in such a way that the evocation of woman as pure image seems necessary and unavoidable.

Memory, in *Fragment of an Empire,* is not a simple process through which a past is remembered so that life can go on as usual. Memory is work, a complex process in which the two terms of past and present can be defined only in a constant state of reciprocal change. If the central opposition in the film is between the past and the present, both in individual and social terms, other oppositions emerge from Fillimonov's search for the one missing link with his own past. When Fillimonov arrives in the city, we recognize in his reactions to these new surroundings not just a man who is recovering from a memory loss, but also the confusion of someone from the country arriving in the city for the first time. The woman's present husband preaches, presumably, the necessity for imagination in revolutionary art and culture; yet he lives his own life in a highly traditional manner. And, as I have suggested, the difference between male and female, between "masculine" aggression and "feminine" nurturance, is central to the film.

In the concluding scene of *Fragment of an Empire,* the woman makes a move to leave with her former husband, but she changes her mind. As Fillimonov leaves the apartment, the woman sobs that this is "the end." Fillimonov faces the camera, speaking directly, and tells the audience that no, this is just the beginning; there is still "much left to be done" (fig. 5.9). This concluding image could be read as a refusal to enclose the film in a fictional self-sufficient universe, emphasizing in a very literal sense the communication between film and audience. Or, conversely, the image might be read as a

Fig.   5.9

refusal to conclude the film in the perhaps expected terms of "man and woman live happily ever after." I think that this conclusion is more appropriately read as a sign of inco-herence, incoherence in the sense that many of the issues raised in the film cannot be wrapped up neatly in a narrative conclusion. The direct address is an attempt to engage Soviet film spectators as, first and foremost, historical subjects and agents of socialist change. Yet, given the problematic status of woman as image in the film, *Fragment of an Empire* can only do so by addressing those spectators as male.

6. *Man with a Movie Camera* and Woman's Work

THERE ARE important differences between the films examined thus far. But when compared with Vertov's 1929 film *Man with a Movie Camera,* in which stunning uses of montage establish complex analogies between production, collectivity, and filmmaking, all of the films discussed in previous chapters suddenly appear to be quite similar. For however different their perspectives on men and women, on the private and the public, on nature and society, these films share a similar narrative common denominator. Eisenstein's narrative structures may be more complex and far-reaching than those of Pudovkin, but when compared with Vertov's film, these differences appear to be less significant, and rather like differences on a narrative continuum. In contrast, Vertov was opposed to any attempts to modify or appropriate artistic forms which, in his view, were better discarded. Hence, while all of the films considered in previous chapters correspond to what I have called a dialectics of appropriation, Vertov's view is better described as a dialectics of emancipation. However, the woman question is as relevant to *Man with a Movie Camera* as it is to other films of the 1920s; the desire to emancipate the production of cinematic meaning in the film relies crucially on a gender component. To be sure, the woman question is posed differently in *Man with a Movie Camera* than it is in other films of the 1920s, but it informs just as persistently and ubiquitously the utopian vision of socialism and of filmmaking present in Vertov's film. *Man with a Movie Camera* is by far the most radically innovative and the most avant-garde of the films under consideration here. It has been an implicit assumption of much feminist criticism that only an avant-garde cinema which challenges and questions the hierarchical relations of the look and of narrative structure can provide a truly alternative form of visual pleasure.[1] Such cases have been made, with varying degrees of success, for avant-garde films informed by the theoretical insights of feminism.[2] However, avant-garde films which are not thus informed remain in a kind of critical limbo, and I would argue that *Man with a Movie Camera* is just such a film—a film whose radical, innovative structure and style have not been addressed adequately in terms of the gender questions that they raise. I am aware that for many critics, gender and the woman question remain suspiciously evocative of what Barthes calls the readerly (*le lisible*); that is, symptoms of an allegiance to a coherent political signified, and to the moralism of the attendant assumption that texts can be readily divided into the categories of "good" and "bad."[3] In other words, a common critical wisdom would have it that the radical process of signification developed in Vertov's film transcends, refuses, or otherwise departs from the universe of binary opposition supposedly inhabited by questions of gender and sexual politics. Now I do not doubt that such critical gestures of transcendence, refusal or departure are often, and perhaps usually, defenses against feminist inquiry, and in particular against the feminist insight that most notions of transcendence (or refusal, or departure) assume or disguise, rather than challenge, the centrality of the male subject. Having said this, I would agree nonetheless that *Man with a Movie Camera* raises many more complex questions concerning cinema, narrative, and gender than do other films of the period. But I take this as an indication, not that Vertov's film stands somehow above and apart from other films in which the woman question functions so centrally, but rather that the woman question is posed in extremely complex and far-reaching ways in the film.

Put another way, I suspect that to many contemporary viewers, *Man with a Movie Camera* would appear to be the film most resistant to the kinds of considerations central to this book, not only because of its formal complexity, but also because of its legendary and critical status as a paragon of cinematic *écriture.* As my previous discussion of the claims of *écriture* in relation to Eisenstein's work should make clear, however, I do not think it possible, in Soviet film of the 1920s, to relegate questions of gender and sexual opposition to secondary or purely "referential" status. I am arguing, then, that *Man with a Movie Camera* is a film which demonstrates, along with other films of the period, the relationship between cinema, narrative and the woman question; and, simultaneously, that Vertov's film raises different questions than do the other films about that relationship.

If the majority of Soviet films of the 1920s develop narrative strategies to represent issues central to socialist culture, it seems then appropriate to conclude with an examination of a film such as *Man with a Movie Camera,* which appears to be so at odds with any such reshaping or redefinition of film narrative. For different reasons, Vertov is the *enfant terrible* of revolutionary Soviet cinema in his own time as well as in our own. While the charge of "formalism" was leveled against many filmmakers, Vertov was particularly susceptible to it, given his determined stance on the politics of socialist filmmaking. And for Eisenstein, of course, *Man with a Movie Camera* consisted of "formalist jackstraws and unmotivated camera mischief."[4] Vertov's position within film history reflects the complex intertwining of political and aesthetic concerns that shaped his own career, and *Man with a Movie Camera,* described by Michelson as "the synthetic articulation of the Marxist project, concretized in every detail of an unprecedented complexity of cinematic design," is the single film that has come to best represent Vertov's radical explorations in socialist cinema.[5] Michelson's exploration of the work of filmmaking in *Man with a Movie Camera,* ranging from magic to epistemology, makes a convincing case for the necessary links between avant-garde practice and Marxist analysis in Vertov's film.[6] And from another perspective, Vertov's importance in the formulation of a relationship between politics and cinematic form is suggested by the interest which his work inspired in the aftermath of the events of May 1968 in France. Indeed, Jean-Luc Godard's adoption of the name "Groupe Dzigna Vertov" for the collective responsible for films such as *Luttes en Italie* (1969) and *Pravda* (1971) suggests that, however enduring the lessons of Eisenstein and other Soviet filmmakers of the silent era, the work of Vertov is more consistently and persistently radical in its insistence on the crucial role of filmmaking in the construction of a socialist view of the world. Indeed, if the emergence of the "Groupe Dzigna Vertov" in France is symptomatic at all, it is in terms of the revalorization of the emancipatory view of the role of the cinema, with the attendant devalorization of Eisenstein as a director compromised by an essentially bourgeois view of the world.[7] In the post-1968 French context, however, Vertov's emblematic status had less to do with the opposition of proletarian and bourgeois—even the most circuitous political logic would be hard pressed to define a film like *British Sounds* (1969) as a proletarian film—than with the opposition between cinema understood as a vehicle for revolutionary change, and cinema understood as a political apparatus in its own right.

However different *Man with a Movie Camera* is from the other Soviet films considered thus far, there still are powerful connections between them. Vertov went further, perhaps, than his colleagues in examining the place of filmmaking in relationship to the productive labor of socialist society. Central to *Man with a Movie Camera* is the relationship, not only between filmmaking and labor, but also between the different gendered spaces of Soviet society. In some ways, *Man with a Movie Camera* seems to center on women as the privileged signifiers of Soviet culture's celebration of work, community, and technology. The figure of the cameraman, whether cranking the camera or peering through its lens, appears at some points in the film to affirm sexual polarity (for instance, by examining the female body in ways coded for voyeurism and sexual display), at other points to put difference into question, and at still other points to suggest a utopian, almost androgynous fusion of male and female as characteristic of Soviet society. The purpose of my analysis, then, is to explore both whether Vertov's differences from his fellow filmmakers of the silent era extend to a difference in representation concerning sexuality and gender, and how the radical process that so many critics have claimed for Vertov extends to the dynamics of gender. My analysis of *Man with a Movie Camera* begins with a consideration of the film's organization, particularly insofar as the film explores the relationships between cinematic production and the productivity of Soviet society, and between perception and representation. At this initial level of analysis, the relevance of the woman question will not be apparent immediately, but the structure of the film raises further questions which require a consideration of gender and sexual opposition. I start with an analysis of the formal structure of the film in order to demonstrate, in other words, the insufficiency of an analysis of *Man with a Movie Camera* in which questions of gender are not taken into account.

Man with a Movie Camera is above all an analysis of movement: the cameraman's movements as he films a population which awakens, goes to work, goes to the beach, engages in sports, listens to music; the movements of the film editor as she cuts and organizes the film strips; the movements of spectators who watch a film, and watch themselves being filmed and watching a film. The orchestration of movement is complex to the point that it is difficult to determine where one movement begins and another leaves off. Each movement is inscribed and defined within the context of another, so that a constant flux is created. The analysis of movement as central to cinematic production is thus inextricably linked to the analysis of social production as labor and as ideology.

Man with a Movie Camera can be divided into five major sections, each structured by relationships central to the process of cinematic production. *Man with a Movie Camera* opens with a shot of the instruments of film production. The cameraman climbs to the top of a gigantic camera behind which are clouds and small hill. He sets up his camera and aims. The second image, a building with clouds moving by rapidly in the background, the viewer assumes, is the image filmed by the cameraman. The "how" precedes the "what"; the image is designated as a product of the cinematic process, and not as a reflection of a world outside that of the film. The following two shots repeat a similar pattern with slight differences. In shot three, the cameraman is seen at an increased distance; and the angle of shot four, a lamppost, is slightly different from the angle of shot two. A puzzling reversal occurs as well: the off-center but nonetheless continuous match between shots one and two is impossible between shots three and four, since in shot three the cameraman picks up his equipment and moves off-screen. Thus, a sense of continuity is established and violated at the same time.

Effects of discontinuity aside, however, the organization of the opening four shots follows a pattern of alternating images. The film as a whole is built on an identical pattern. The first four shots depict the instruments of film production and the resulting images. A shift in emphasis occurs in shot five, where the cameraman walks through a curtain. Subsequent shots suggest that this is a stage curtain in a movie theater. Then a movie theater is seen, preparing for a film screening. Spectators enter and take their seats, the projectionist sets up, and musicians prepare to begin their accompaniment. Here, there is a relationship established between the spectator and the means by which images are perceived: the projector and the movie screen, most obviously, but also the accoutrements of film viewing such as music and the accommodations of the theater. Hence, from the outset, *Man with a Movie Camera* sets up a series of opposing terms: filmmaker and image, on the one hand; and viewer and film on the other.

With the appearance of the number "1" on the screen, the film within the film (seen by the spectators in the theater) coincides with the film that has already begun. The emphasis then shifts to the underlying relationship of the first section of the film, between images and the instruments of film production. This relationship undergoes a number of reversals, pauses, and visual parentheses, but a fundamental organizational link is maintained between the chronology of a day in the life of a Soviet city, and the activities of the filmmaker as he produces this chronology. The extension of the first part of the film constitutes the largest portion of *Man with a Movie Camera.*

A vertiginous sequence of superpositions, rapid editing, and split images of Soviet citizens listening to and making music marks the final segment of this part of the film. Music defined the transition from the second section of the film, concerned with the conditions of watching a film, to the third, concerned, as is the first section, with the conditions of producing a film. Music also defines the transition from the third to the fourth section of the film, in which the relationship between spectator and film is central. The film-within-the-film continues and is shot from alternating angles. Images of the film-within-the-film (coinciding with our vision of the screen), of the group of spectators watching the film, and of isolated spectators reacting to it, are constantly interchanged.

Approximately halfway through the fourth section of the film, the movie theater is in preparation for another film to begin. The lights go down, musicians begin to play, and the curtain opens. From this point on, nearly all of the images are repetitions or variations of images that have already been seen in the film. The final segment presents a reassemblage of the principal elements that form the oppositions between and within previous sections of the film. The final moments of *Man with a Movie Camera* are characterized by a dizzying pace of technical virtuosity, in which the film appears to dissect and, to some extent, to undermine, its own structure. In the last shot, a human eye in extreme close-up is reflected in a camera lens, marking a fusion of human perception and cinematic technique. If *Man with a Movie Camera* ends, as any film must, it nonetheless refuses closure in the traditional sense, for the end of the film implies the beginning of another process, a new way of seeing. The conclusion recalls the close-up of the eye at the end of Eisenstein's *Strike*. But, whereas the conclusion of Eisenstein's film serves as a reminder of the connection between historical and cinematic vision, the conclusion of Vertov's film marks the fusion of the human and the technological.

Man with a Movie Camera does not lend itself to the kind of narrative structure breakdown used for the films discussed previously. Indeed, there is something deceptive about the five-part structure of the film that I've described, for *Man with a Movie Camera* resists such linear logic. While the film does begin by representing a series of relationships concerning different aspects of the filmmaking process, there is never a question of film production and film viewing retaining their qualities as separate and distinct moments. Rather, film production and film spectatorship become identified as part of the same process. Alan Williams refers, in this context, to the various "narrative perversions" in *Man with a Movie Camera*, stressing the refusal of the film to preserve the oppositions it establishes. "Vertov's text," writes Williams, "will decompose and pervert cause-and-effect narrativity to rely on formal, logical structures which, rather than support the classic metonymy of the fiction film, will create their own progressions based on difference and juxtaposition."[8]

If *Man with a Movie Camera* does not function as a narrative in the classical sense of the term, the film might be considered as a meta-narrative, that is, a film that tells a story about itself, about the activities of the cameraman rather than about a fictional character. Perhaps the extreme reflexivity and self-consciousness of Vertov's film is reason enough to distinguish him from his contemporaries. From the very beginning, however, the centrality of the cameraman's vision is put into question, since he moves out of frame in the third shot of the film. In other words, the cameraman cannot be equated with a central character, or even the central narrating intelligence of a narrative film, since visual perspective is not localized in a single figure, but dispersed through multiple perspectives. Rather, there is another, more central relationship that structures the entire film, and that is the relationship between perception and representation, with representation understood throughout the film as a process of construction.

Early in the film, when spectators enter the movie theater, two series of images alternate over a brief time span: shots of seats in the theater which "magically" unfold by themselves, and shots of spectators who enter the theater, find their seats, and sit down (folding down the seats themselves). As in the opening four shots of the film, an obvious manipulation of the image contrasts with shots that are more realistic—more "natural." This alternation ends with a shot of one seat unfolding by itself; a woman and small child enter the frame and sit down. Two different modes of representation are condensed in the same image. One emphasizes representation as overt manipulation of the image; the other, as less mediated perception, realistic in its focus. While this event does indeed fit into an ongoing narrative structure, that structure is interrupted constantly by an exploration of how individual events might be dissected and analyzed. Similarly, while there certainly is a narrative chronology in the film ("a day in the life of a Soviet city"), it is a chronology that seems to function more as a vehicle for the analysis of movement than as a center of narrative interest in its own right.

However, it is a mistake, I think, to assume that all traces of narrative are banished from *Man with a Movie Camera*. Rather, the film is characterized by a tension between narration, understood as an illusory ordering of space and time, and production, understood as a laying-bare of that illusion. This is not to say that Vertov's film is, therefore, a narrative in the same way as the other films that have been examined. What marks the difference in *Man with a Movie Camera*, when seen in relationship to other films of the 1920s, is its emphasis on a principle of production. At the same time, *Man with a Movie Camera* is distinctive within the context of the 1920s, not because it is a nonnarrative film but because it is a different kind of narrative film. While all the films I have examined are structured by the narrative opposition of "us" and "them," of proletariat and bourgeois, *Man with a Movie Camera* assumes that opposition, and moves into the presumably new signifying territory made possible by socialism. *Man with a Movie Camera* is characterized by a distinctly utopian vision of the cinema as well as of socialist society, a vision of supreme harmony and integration.

Michelson describes the structural center of *Man with a Movie Camera* as the alternation between images of the components of a textile factory and the image of the cameraman who films a hydroelectric plant and mines, the sources of power for the factory. The alternation builds to a superimposition of the cameraman over an image of a woman tending to a machine in the textile factory. Of the relationship thus articulated between filmmaking and textile production, Michelson writes:

This juxtaposition and subsequent superimposition of filmmaking and textile manufacture are to be read as articulating that unity within which the "natural" inequalities and contradictions formerly generated by a system of division of labor have been suspended. The full range of analogical and metaphorical readings thereby generated signify a general and organic unity, a common implication within the movement of industry, the euphoric and intensified sense of a shared end: the supercession of private property in the young socialist state under construction.[9]

Implicit in Michelson's analysis of the sequence in question is, perhaps, yet another unity, although she does not address it per se. This is, of course, the unity of male and female, drawn here as a configuration of equals, with the classic status of woman as *image* broken in favor of woman identified as agent of production. Although Williams characterizes *Man with a Movie Camera* in terms different from Michelson, he also suggests that the film is utopian in another, related sense, as it militates against the trappings of bourgeois narrative. In defense of his claim that *Man with a Movie Camera* "is to be read not as narrative but as conflict," Williams cites the film's use of point-of-view structures. "Nowhere in the film," writes Williams, "is there an unambiguous use of this common alternation: the seer is never in the same textual space as the seen." Williams cites the example of the athletic sequences in the film, "where slow motion athletes are 'seen' by spectators shot at normal speed and who furthermore look in the 'wrong' direction for good matching."[10] It is by now a truism of film theory and film analysis that the organization of the look through shot reverse-shot and point-of-view shots is structured by gender difference.[11] While most analyses of the male gaze and its attendant implications for the representation of the female body take as their point of departure the classical Hollywood film, the cinema was structured by the hierarchy of sexual difference long before the development of the Hollywood film, and in other national contexts.[12] Williams's claims for the use of point-of-view structures might be taken a bit further. Even though Vertov's cinematic innovations and explorations have not been read widely in terms of the issues of gender that they raise, Williams's designation of the "ambiguous" use of the point-of-view structure suggests, especially when seen in the light of how that structure has been analyzed by feminist critics, that *Man with a Movie Camera* is as involved with the notion of process in sexual terms as it is in ideological, social, and technological terms.

In other words, the central question I wish to ask of *Man with a Movie Camera* is how the relationships of gender—of man and woman in a socialist context, certainly, but also of those qualities which, whether through cultural association or through textual production, are designated "male" and "female"—inform the radical vision of process, conflict, and production. The examples cited above from Michelson and Williams are both suggestive, in different ways, of a radical vision of sexual politics that informs Vertov's exploration of the "communist decoding of the world."[13] If indeed this is the case, then Vertov would appear to have achieved something that eluded his contemporaries, the conscious and deliberate articulation of a necessary connection between gender and social formation.

In order to examine in detail how a gender dynamic func-

tions in *Man with a Movie Camera,* I will look at a crucial
sequence where two different moments in the process of filmmaking are set up in relationship to each other. Not coinci-
dentally, the principals in this sequence are the cameraman
(portrayed in the film by Vertov's brother), and the editor,
portrayed by Vertov's real-life wife, editor and collaborator,
Elizaveta Svilova. This sequence occurs approximately one-
third of the way into the film. In the midst of a sequence in
which the cameraman films carriages in motion, the movement of the carriages is suspended in a series of frozen shots,
and is later resumed after other frozen or motionless images,
drawn from different points of reference in the film, become
illustrations for the stages of film editing.

There are four moments of cinematic production depicted
in *Man with a Movie Camera*: the cameraman and the shooting
of film footage; the camera itself, which is seen at crucial
moments in the film as a perceptual apparatus detached from
the cameraman's control; editing; and the act of viewing a
film. These moments are not depicted chronologically, suggesting that they constitute relationships that inform the en-
tirety of the cinematic experience. These different aspects of
cinematic production also become metaphoric points of
departure. Cinema is labor, hence similar to the work of
machines in the numerous factory segments of the film. In
more general terms, cinema is linked to the structural patterns
of the games and sports Soviets play and watch, and the music
they listen to. Cinema is like these activities, but cinema is also
given a special function as the medium that alone is capable of
producing the representation of analogy, of the similarity of
motion and of structure. This view of the cognitive capacity of
cinema assumes that, as a technological form, cinema is capable of changing significantly the nature of human perception.
Such an assumption cuts across two contexts: cinema as a representational form that simultaneously demystifies, and cine-

ma as part of a social whole, the context in which any change—perceptual or otherwise—ultimately is defined.

Like other Soviet filmmakers of his time, Vertov considered montage both the essence of cinematic form and the foundation of cinema as a dialectical medium. Thus it is not surprising that a demonstration of editing occupies a special position in *Man with a Movie Camera*. The camera, the act of filming, and film viewing are all depicted in the film from the outset. It is not until somewhat later, however, that editing is demonstrated, and in a sequence that is set off from the rest of the film (that is, "set off" to the limited extent that anything is set off in Vertov's film). Hence, given this special role assigned to editing, the four major aspects of cinematic production initially appear to be separated according to an opposition between perception (the camera, the filmmaker, and the film spectator) and construction (the film editor).

The editing sequence consists of five segments, each of which demonstrates a specific function of montage. The first segment consists of nine stills, the first four of which are repetitions from the carriage sequence immediately preceding. Although movement is frozen, linear continuity is preserved. Shot five, a frozen long shot of a city street full of people, has not been seen in the film. However, similar shots of city streets are used in *Man with a Movie Camera* as a means of indicating the progression of a day's activities, with the amount of activity and the number of people present indicating the time of day. This is the first image of its kind to signify a city at the peak of activity. Just as the basic element in the representation of motion and movement in film is a single motionless frame, so the height of a city's activity is represented by a still shot.

The four images which follow repeat the familiar pattern of alternating montage. Two shots of peasant women, their heads in scarves and facing screen right, alternate with two shots of little girls wearing bows in their hair and facing screen

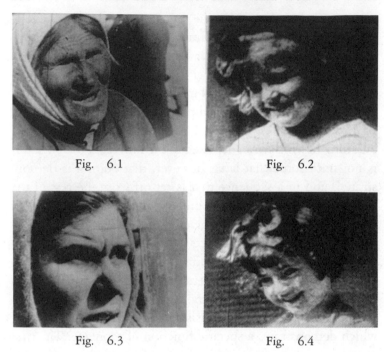

Fig. 6.1   Fig. 6.2

Fig. 6.3   Fig. 6.4

left (figs. 6.1–6.4). The first peasant woman appeared earlier. However, recognition of the image is not as immediate as recognition of images of the carriages or of the city street, because the image appeared relatively quickly, and it does not have the same foregrounded function. The second peasant woman appears in this sequence for the first time, as do the children who reappear much later in the film as spectators at a magic show on the beach. While these four images have different points of reference (the past, present, and future tenses of the film), they are linked here by a repetition of the central structuring device, the alternating montage pattern. Thus, we perceive continuity of movement as both presence and as illusion. The demonstration of illusion is taken another step further, beyond simple frozen motion: the images of the little girls are filmstrips, with sprocket holes clearly visible. Cinematic time is the function of cinematic space, itself broken down into two separate components, the space of the screen and the space of the filmstrip. The first segment of the sequence, consisting of these nine shots, is informed by a principle of laying bare cinematic space and time. Cinematic space is reduced to the boundaries of the filmstrip, and cinematic time, to the individual photogram.

The second segment of the sequence consists of two images of rolls of film classified on shelves. These images recall the rolls of film shown when the projectionist loads the projector to begin the film-within-the-film. In that scene, attention is drawn as well to the isolated image on the filmstrip, a window which later appears immediately after the number "1" appears on screen. A chronology of the status of the image is sketched, from the reel of film to the single photogram to the image in movement on the screen. Here, in the editing sequence, the same principle occurs in reverse, from image in motion, to single image on the filmstrip, to rolls of film. The reversal is important on other levels as well. The earlier scene suggests, at the very least, the kind of voyeuristic fascination that has been central to the cinema since its earliest years of development—what else is an image of a window, if not an invitation to explore what lies within its frame? That the projectionist is male, and the person whose waking rituals (within what is assumed to be the same room) are witnessed is female, suggests the classic structure of the man who looks and the woman who is looked at. However, what is more difficult and more crucial to assess is the perspective from which such a voyeuristic structure is put into place. The relationship is in no way naturalized; that is, the projectionist may well be a figure of mastery and control, but control is directed toward the technology of cinema. But it surely is no coincidence that technology and the female body function as subject and object, respectively. However distanced and demystified, the structure presented still maintains the traditional contours of the man who controls the image, and the woman who *is* the image. When the relationship between filmstrip, film reel, and moving image is again articulated in the editing room sequence, it appears as though the voyeuristic configurations of the previous scene are being thrown into question. A woman's gaze replaces a man's, and the filmstrips of the little girls replace the frame within the frame of the window on the filmstrip. There is still an association between inert material and female identity, but the association is complicated by the fact that the active agent in the editing sequence is also a woman.

Between the isolated, frozen images that occur at the beginning of the editing sequence and the rolls of film classified on shelves, ready to be edited into a film, some type of work occurs, such as the threading of the projector which allows the transformation of the filmstrip into the image in motion. The third segment of the sequence demonstrates this work, which is a bridge between the images inscribed by the cameraman and the images that the editor classifies, and between those images and the ways in which they are organized in the film. In segment three, a series of images depicts the basic materials with which the editor works: a motionless take-up reel, photograms of a plump peasant woman (fig. 6.5), and the filmstrip being wound onto the reel. The editor is seen operating the take-up reel (fig. 6.6) and, in close-up, cutting the film. Finally, the filmstrip is transformed. An eyeline direction match unites the image of the peasant woman and the editor as she examines the filmstrip. The filmstrip then "comes alive," its boundaries redefined as identical to those of the screen (figs. 6.7–6.9). Three aspects of cinematic production are separated, and each is identified as part of yet another process. The illustration of the editor's materials gives indications of the method used; and the illustration of cutting indicates, through the eyeline direction match, what the product will be. Such a fusion

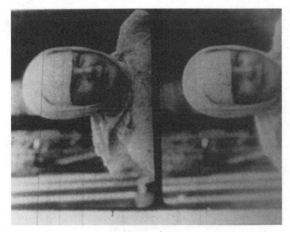

Fig.   6.5

Fig.   6.6

Fig. 6.7

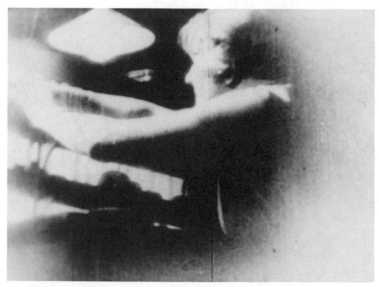

Fig. 6.8

Fig.   6.9

of method and material suggests a constant process and not a resolution in the form of a final product.

The fourth segment of the sequence reiterates the work of editing in shorthand form, showing editor, filmstrip, and image in motion. The images transformed are those of children who, like the little girls seen earlier as photograms, reappear later. Thus the work of editing, previously demonstrated on an image which appears nowhere else in the film, here becomes defined more immediately within the narrative of the film. This integration of editing into the text of the film continues in segment five. Two frozen images of the old woman and a city street are the same images seen in segment one. These frozen images alternate with the same images in motion, and the editor appears less frequently. These images return us to the narrative context of the film, yet they function simultaneously as objects, as pieces of raw material that are transformed. Hence representation is defined as the process of transformation

rather than as reflection. Finally, the carriage sequence re-
commences. In extreme light and dark contrast, the editor's
hand moves over a filmstrip, on which the image is unreada-
ble. Hence, the reestablishment of so-called normal continuity
is accompanied by intense abstraction, for this image could be
any image, and the moment of transformation, any moment.
The continuation of the carriage sequence is interrupted
again by an image of the take-up reel, now moving rapidly
and bearing a full roll of film. The reel defines the duration of
the editing sequence, like the shots of city streets that function
as temporal markers. Thus the take-up reel marks the time of
the projection of *Man with a Movie Camera*. Finally, the cameraman walks down a street. The sequence continues as he
moves on to other activities.

It is significant that in the editing sequence filmstrips are
cut, looked at, and classified, but never fused together. Montage is Vertov's principle of construction, understood both as
putting things together and as taking them apart. Elements
may be brought together in one direction, only to be taken
apart in another. Thus montage cannot be equated with a
single technique. Vertov's writings on the function of montage
might appear to be simple ecstasizing on the virtues of the
"pure cinematic language" the filmmaker sought to elaborate.
Seen in the context of the editing sequence, however, this statement clarifies to what degree montage, for Vertov, cannot be
focused on one particular technique: "Every kino-eye production is subject to montage from the moment the theme is cho-
sen until the film's release in its completed form. In other
words, it is edited during the entire process of film production."[14]

There are elements in the editing sequence that are shared
by the activities of the camera, the filmmaker, and the spectators. The camera aligns itself with human perception to
reveal different structural properties of the objects before it,

and the work of the editor functions similarly to clarify and analyze movement. Also, the editor's relationship to the film is analogous to the relationship between the cameraman and what he films in the preceding carriage sequence. The ways in which the editor views the images are not unlike the ways spectators look at the film screen. The initial separation between perception and construction which marks off the editing sequence serves, then, to redefine more clearly the interdependence of the two terms as inseparable moments of cinematic production. Production is defined in *Man with a Movie Camera* as a multidirectional flow, implying a refusal both to ground the image in one-dimensional reality and to assign it a set of closed meanings.

Yet, for all of Vertov's preoccupation with the circulation of images, and with patterns of continuity that disrupt rather that contain, the editing sequence has surprisingly familiar contours. We see the woman, who works exclusively with images of women and children, in a room. Outside that room is the public sphere of filmmaking—the (male) cameraman and street activity. While the editing room hardly can be described as a private space, there is a spatial tension generated on the basis of interior versus exterior space, female versus male activity. To be sure, it could be argued that *Man with a Movie Camera* poses the opposition only to demolish it. It certainly is true of the film that collectivity reigns supreme, so that what viewers see is the redefinition of the private, isolated space of women in capitalist society into the collective, socialized sphere of women and men in socialist society. Given the constant flow that permeates all levels of *Man with a Movie Camera*, it is tempting to argue that the difference between male and female—between the cameraman and the film editor—becomes a point of departure and a form of differentiation, rather than a fixed reference point of active versus passive, of subject versus object.

Earlier I referred to the parallels between the editing sequence and the previous scene in the film where the projector
is loaded, and the film within the film begins after the appearance of a "1" on the screen. A young woman is awakening in a
room. This is virtually the only private sphere represented in
the film, as if the increasing momentum of *Man with a Movie
Camera* creates a collective cinematic space in which these ves-
tiges of traditional narrative are done away with.[15] In this
scene, close-ups of the camera alternate with images of the
woman's eyes. Her foggy vision is clarified as the scene outside her window moves into crisp focus. Thus, the camera
begins to function as a substitute for (imperfect) human perception. The camera has, at the very least, a two-fold function
here. It is both a point of view within the film, and a substitute
for the woman's own vision. Such a fusion of subject and
object—through the camera, the woman becomes both the
object seen and the perceiving subject—is, perhaps, the most
utopian vision in the film. Now it could be argued that it is
symptomatic of a duality of activity versus passivity, and its
attendant sexual implications, that it be the woman who must
be fused, as it were. At the same time it could be argued that,
because the figure of woman exemplifies objectification, the
fusion of the kino-eye with the woman's perception is a radical demonstration of *Man with a Movie Camera*'s challenge to
cinematic and cultural convention. While it is true that Vertov's film brings questions of gender to the forefront of cinematic signification, the fusion of human and cinematic perception in this particular scene is nonetheless characterized by
the woman's function as other—she is an isolated, apparently
bourgeoise figure in a private space, in a film that celebrates
proletarian collectivity.[16]

A more obvious function of the camera in the film is in
terms of what Seth Feldman calls a "barometer of social
involvement."[17] When the cameraman films Soviets who

awaken and go to work, close-ups of the camera lens alternate with shots of a young man who awakens from a night spent on a park bench. The boy mugs for the camera, conspicuously amused. Immediately following the last image of the boy is a shot of a woman cleaning a city street. The only other conscious mugging for the camera occurs during the carriage sequence. A variety of social classes are represented. An obviously middle-class woman passenger in one of the carriages giggles as she imitates the movements of the cameraman's hands. The camera differentiates between those committed to the work of Soviet society and those extraneous to it. The symmetry here is striking; one person who is aware of the camera is male and presumably subproletarian, another is female and middle-class. While the attempt at equality is admirable, the social function of the camera here is different from the perceptual function discussed above. In the previous case, the camera embodies a desire to incorporate the poles of male and female subjectivity, whereas here sexual division becomes a support for the commentary on class differences.

But the progression of *Man with a Movie Camera* suggests that the desire to incorporate male and female difference within the camera constitutes the larger movement of the film. The filmmaker is often portrayed in a social context, and whatever other cinematic reasons there initially may be to designate the work of film editing as more isolated or privatized, the signifying effect is to create a separation between male and female realms of activity. Film editing first appears in a way marked off from the social arena defining filmmaking and the life of socialist society as a whole. However, the work of the film editor reappears approximately halfway through the film. Through a series of rapidly edited shots, montage is equated quite literally with the productive work of Soviet society. Different forms of labor are shown, including that of the cinema. Alternating images depict two kinds of labor. People beautify themselves, and it surely is significant that both men and women are depicted in this context. One woman has her hair washed, another has makeup applied, a man gets a shave, a woman has her hair cut and styled, and another gets a manicure. Alternating with these images is another kind of labor. Clothes are washed, an axe is sharpened, shoes are shined, and mud is thrown on a building. Each juxtaposition of images is determined by movement and direction matches. The formal continuity is disrupted by the opposition between productive labor and the pains taken for the purpose of beautification. Shots of the camera and the filmmaker begin to replace the images of productive labor, equating the two and implying that filmmaking is also antithetical to the work of superfluous decoration. A similar opposition underlies an alternation between a manicure session and the film editor as she, in movements formally similar to those of the manicurist's hands, prepares to join pieces of film together.

I would not disagree with Williams when he writes:

The motions of a beauty parlor are compared with the cranking of a movie camera, to various machines in a factory, to a lower-class woman washing a wall. But the similarity of these actions and their placement at the same time of day in the (pseudo-) narrative continuity serve to underline a difference between the productive work of the working classes and useless expenditure of energy by the bourgeoisie."[18]

I take Williams's remarks as a reminder that however tempting it might be to evaluate *Man with a Movie Camera* in terms purely of cinematic *écriture*, of the dizzying free play of signifiers, this is a film which exists within a political context. I would argue that the structural similarities between beauty parlors and filmmaking are certainly meant to be undercut by the enormous differences that separate them, but that the process of differentiation is not completely convincing. For an image of a man getting a shave notwithstanding, the term of comparison here is first and foremost the feminine—a world of closed spaces, of self-absorption and of preoccupation with decoration and display. To be sure, this is a world designated as bourgeois, and throughout the film there has been a differentiation between proletarian and bourgeois primarily through the representation of women. As Stephen Crofts and Olivia Rose point out, there is a contrast between "the perfunctory hair-combing of the women leaving work" and "the satire's constant return to cosmetics, manicuring, etc., an industry whose targets are women."[19]

My point is not that Vertov's film relies on sexual duality in its attempt to articulate a vision of the collective strength of socialist society, and that the vision of collectivity in the film is, therefore, compromised by a resurrection of sexual hierarchy. Nor am I arguing that this sexual opposition somehow "undermines" *Man with a Movie Camera.* Indeed, it could be argued that the strength of the film lies precisely in its recognition and articulation of the difficulty presented by "woman" in any social discourse—whether it be capitalist or socialist. What I wish to stress, rather, is that in articulating a vision of the intertwining elements of socialist society, the points of difficulty, of tension, are virtually always associated with women. True, the opposition between proletarian and sub-proletarian occurs primarily through the representation of men, but this opposition occupies relatively little screen time. *Man with a Movie Camera* presents a utopian view of collectivity, in which the forthright analogies between cinema and labor are accompanied by other analogies that are far more ambivalent. The film distinguishes between women on the basis of class, and enthusiastically represents women workers as the embodiments of socialism. In the continuation of the "beauty versus labor" scene described above, a series of images of a young female worker sewing portrays labor in a more organic, less fragmented way. Unlike previous shots, where workers were portrayed in more partial fashion, the focus here is on the worker in more complete terms. Then, the focus on the individual worker shifts to images of collective work in the textile factory. Finally, images of the textile factory alternate with shots of the editor; movement and direction matches unite the two series of images. Film editing is thus equated with social practice, and in the series of images that follow, machines, the camera, and the film editor are interwoven in a dizzying montage that conveys the height of the day's production.

In another section of the film, however, the traits of femininity are not so easily integrated into the flow of socialist production. Approximately halfway through the film, couples are filmed in an administrative office filing for marriage, divorce, and declarations of birth. Suddenly the emphasis shifts to become much broader, and the human life cycle is represented in condensed form: a woman cries over a grave, a funeral proceeds down a street, a newly married couple steps into a carriage, a woman gives birth. The theme of the human life cycle is introduced on a cut from a couple in the office filling out a birth declaration form to an old woman crying over a grave. The woman in the first shot is wearing a white scarf, and out of shyness (it is assumed), she covers her face (fig. 6.10). The elderly woman in the second shot also wears a scarf, and covers her face in exactly the same manner. Hence, the headdress provides the match to connect two different emotions, timidity and grief. But there is also a more obvious connection between the shots, and that is the display of emotional responses. The scarf motif is carried throughout the series, so that, when a bride and groom descend from a carriage, it is the woman who becomes foregrounded as the principle of continuity, and when a woman gives birth, the towel draped across her head places childbirth within a formal,

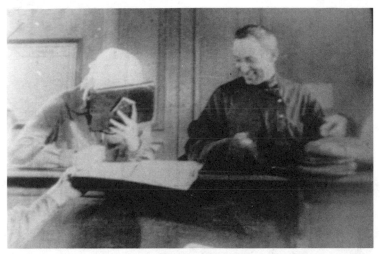

Fig.   6.10

cinematic pattern of production and reproduction. The accoutrements of female identity—clothing, gesture, the expression of emotion—become the signs upon which the representation of the human life cycle is based.

Woman in *Man with a Movie Camera* functions on one level as a kind of figural excess, most frequently associated with class distinctions, but also—as in the representation of the human life cycle—in terms that are not reducible to class determinations. The film creates a vision of socialist society where men and women, and male and female positions, are as interconnected as the camera lens and the process of editing. Yet, while *Man with a Movie Camera* puts forth this utopian vision, that vision is complicated by the exploration of the foundations—ideological as well as formal—of cinematic representation. Woman functions in a more complex way in *Man with a Movie Camera* than in the other films discussed. But the relationship between subject and object retains the familiar contours of gender polarity. On-the-street filming may well reveal the class divisions that persist in Soviet society, whereby

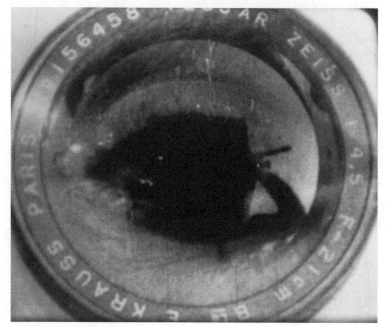

Fig.   6.11

some Soviet citizens—captured as they awake from a night
spent on a park bench—do not have the comforts of a home.
When the citizen in question is a woman, however, the class
commentary is submerged by sexual objectification, with the
woman's body fragmented by the distinctly and eagerly male
point of view of the camera (figs. 6.11 and 6.12). Certainly,
Man with a Movie Camera celebrates an ostensibly new eroticism
of the fusion of human perception and the cinematic machine,
but one cannot help but remark upon the persistence with
which the woman's body remains the object of that perception.
And the woman in the white scarf, shielding her face from the
camera while her male companion chuckles, suggests, if not a
resistance to being filmed, at the very least a discomfort with
the social and technological function of the cinema so enthusiastically embraced in *Man with a Movie Camera*.

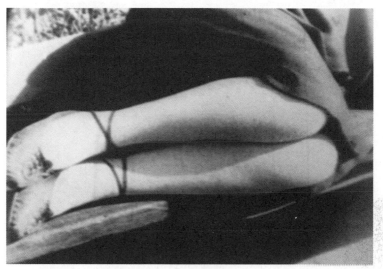

Fig.   6.12

Afterword

MY ANALYSES of Soviet films of the 1920s are meant to be provocative to the extent that they claim, for feminism, the relevance of a group of films that otherwise has been measured in terms of either academic or political concerns from which questions of gender are by and large banished or marginalized to the area of "secondary contradiction." However, it is not my purpose in this book to make claims, in the name of feminism, for the progressive vision of one film versus the reactionary vision of another. The complexity of Soviet films, as well as the complexity of the period from which they emerged, make it extremely difficult to attribute one single vision of gender and sexual politics to an individual film, much less ascribe that vision plus or minus points on the scale of political correctness. And in any case, political correctness does not go very far as a criterion for analysis. Of all the films that have been examined in previous chapters, Pudovkin's *Mother* seems to me the most simplistic, the most straightforward, and—in terms of the issues of gender that it raises—the most problematic film in its engagement with the woman question. As I have argued, *Mother* is a film about the son more than it is about the mother, and the political trajectory that the film follows does not in any way challenge the traditional role of motherhood. Put another way, there is only one position available to the woman as a central narrative figure, and that is in the conventional role of mother. Now, I think it is tempting to assume that it is precisely because of its cine-

matic and narrative straightforwardness and simplicity that
Mother is so problematic; to assume, in other words, that those
films which engage only superficially or reluctantly with the
complexities of cinematic representation are doomed to per-
petuate, rather than challenge, the hierarchies of gender.
However, in some ways *Mother* articulates quite clearly something that is present in all films of the period, and that is the
difficulty of identifying a woman as the subject of the film—
subject understood as the narrative and discursive center of
the film, and not just the woman as protagonist. Ironically,
perhaps, among those films I have discussed, the one that
comes the closest to identifying its subject as female is *Bed and
Sofa;* however lacking *Bed and Sofa* may be in formal complexity, it nonetheless explores the complex narrative and visual
implications of sexual hierarchy.

Anyone who has followed the development of literary and
film criticism over the last two decades is aware that it is not
only extremely unfashionable, but also embarrassingly naïve,
to speak of "form" and "content." Pronouncements of critics
about signifying practice and the heterogeneous production
of meaning notwithstanding, I am not convinced that contemporary criticism has departed as radically as one might think
from the idealist and mechanistic assumptions of "form" versus "content." It seems that a recurrent feature of discussions
of Soviet cinema of the 1920s is the assumption, however
unconscious, of a split between the political codes of the films
and their formal innovations. I am not speaking here of the
familiar academicism which praises the form and bemoans
the content, but rather of a short-circuited argument whereby
a political avant-gardism is forged on the sole basis of the
formal experimentation of the films, an experimentation
which is presumed to create stunning new articulations of
political process and subject positioning.

The consolidation of avant-garde practice and political radicalism is commonly associated with a certain moment in the development of French theories of representation and signification. Soviet films of the 1920s were rediscovered and reread with great enthusiasm in the early 1970s, since they seemed to offer the promise of formal experimentation within a socialist context. Put another way, Soviet films of the 1920s allowed you to have your cake and eat it, to embrace the plurality and *jouissance* of textual practice, and not only to avoid the dreaded epithet of bourgeois formalism, but to claim socialist credentials at the same time. To be sure, discussions of textual practice coincided with other, more familiar debates, such as the disagreement between Eisenstein and Vertov, which pitted one film journal, *Cahiers du cinéma* (in which Eisenstein was the *cause célèbre*), against another, *Cinéthique* (which claimed to follow Vertov's example). The work of Ropars, Sorlin, and Michèle Lagny on Eisenstein's *October* is, perhaps, the most striking example of the rediscovery of Soviet film of the 1920s. Their collective work on Eisenstein's *October* began with the publication of *October: Ecriture et idéologie* in 1976, with the second volume, *La Révolution Figurée: Film, histoire, politique* following in 1979. The title of the second volume suggests the kind of claims to which I refer, claims articulated in the following terms in the introduction to the volume:

The notion of figure occurs at the intersection of a certain number of questions. In the first place, *October* is a figure by virtue of one of the principal materials of the filmic text, the image, considered as a figuration analogous to the real. In more radical terms, Eisenstein's film, as an operation of language, relies on figural representation in its intrinsic ambiguity: the Revolution, understood as a specific category of historical process, takes shape (*prend figure*) in the rhetorical form of narrative; the narrative sometimes is undone by opening itself up to movements which we will call figural, to the extent that they abolish any possibility of assigning figuration to previously-established codes, and thus of establishing a revolutionary model.[1]

While this attempt to come to terms with the "intrinsic ambiguity" of figural representation is admirable, that ambiguity never seems to stray far from political radicalism.[2] *La Révolution Figurée* is divided into two rather distinct sections, the first is a detailed reading of the temporal structure of *October,* and the second is an examination of the relationship between the diegetic and figural levels of the film insofar as they articulate ideological conflict. It might be tempting to say that this separation reinforces the distinction between analyses focused on formal versus historical questions; however, this detailed analysis of *October* cannot be categorized quite that easily. What I find problematic about the claims that are made for a filmmaker, such as Eisenstein, in the name of an emancipatory cinematic *écriture,* is that figural tensions and ambiguities within his films are immediately assigned a positive function and are designed as "radical" inscriptions. To be sure, this is a notion of radical politics that is considerably more sophisticated and complex than, and preferable to, the formulae of socialist realism or the master narrative of good proletarians versus evil capitalists, but it is no less problematic. The problem is not that radical claims are made for certain strategies of cinematic representation, but rather that those claims are made so univocally and monolithically. Put another way, there is something just as mechanistic about an immediate association between figural process and radical subjectivity as there is about the one-dimensional allegiance to a political signified.

I do not want to define feminism as a reality principle that will shatter these utopian premises; that is, I do not wish to erect feminist perspectives as the new master codes, as new truth factors, that will undo and undermine the claims that have been made for the radical and innovative experimentation of Soviet film. Rather, a feminist perspective on Soviet film of the 1920s suggests that formal ambiguity and textual play cannot be located definitively or unproblematically within a textual politics of radical subjectivity; too often ambiguity and play rely on the position of woman defined in a decidely unradical way. Once again, this is not to deny the possibility of a Soviet cinematic practice that poses new possibilities for subject positioning and narrative desire, but rather to insist that such possibilities are themselves posed in contradictory ways.

I can imagine arguments quite different than those advanced in this book concerning the textual details upon which are constructed problematic articulations of the woman question. Perhaps it could be argued that the structural equivalence between women and spies in Eisenstein's *Strike* serves to problematize the marginality of women, or that the visual pattern of speckles of light shining on the faces of the man and the woman in close-up in *Bed and Sofa* undermines sexual hierarchy. Or it might even be argued that in *Mother,* the relationship between human beings and the cycles of nature is defamiliarized, or put into question. Such arguments as these might be attentive to the feminine, that is, to what is represented within male-centered representation, but they are inattentive to issues of gender and sexual politics, that is, to the implications of such repressions for constructions of female identity and relations of power. What feminism brings to the study of Soviet film is a healthy skepticism about what seems to me a kind of textual idealism. Textual details, such as the peculiar affinity drawn between the obnoxious cultural worker and Fillimonov in *Fragment of an Empire* through the match cut near the conclusion of the film, or the peculiarly ambivalent inflection given the ostensible opposition between the superfluous labor of the cosmetic industry and the genuine labor of Soviet society in *Man with a Movie Camera,* cannot categorically and immediately be read as symptoms of a radical practice.

It is crucial, however, to insist upon the tension between

textual details and the conflicts generated within the films as far as their class and gender dynamics are concerned. However much one may admire the remarkable achievements of Soviet film style, the films nonetheless function within a fairly rigid master narrative of bourgeoisie versus proletariat. This master narrative is not always the paragon of ideological simplicity or coherence that some would suggest, but neither is it so readily compatible with a free flow of signification. Indeed, the notion of a master narrative is just as susceptible to a kind of idealism as is a devotion to *écriture*. Part of my goal in this study has been to suggest that the various articulations of the woman question demonstrate that, however different they may be in other ways, notions of political coherence and of cinematic *écriture* are extremely precarious formulations.

The woman question complicates these notions in a variety of ways. In *Strike,* women are defined as creatures of private space who confound the neat and clear distinctions drawn in the film between workers and bosses. In figural terms, women belong neither completely to the realm of the diegesis or to the realm of metaphor, but are rather both and neither simultaneously. In *Mother,* a sense of class identity and solidarity is created by a shift in representation of the woman, from oppressive servitude to her husband, to supposed authentic nurturance of her son. In other words, class solidarity is shaped and consolidated by the substitution of one traditional gender role for another. In this film, however, the mother is eliminated fairly quickly from the realm of metaphor in order to define the son as the symbolic and political center of the film, and whatever figural function she has is quickly displaced by her mediating function, between the human world (her son) and the natural world. In *Bed and Sofa,* the persistence of class divisions in contemporary Soviet society is reflected in the hierarchy of sexual division, particularly concerning marriage. In Room's film, spatial relationships assume the function of narrative and visual opposition, with Ludmilla's position by the window becoming a strategic threshold between the realms of private and public life. While the primary focus of *Fragment of an Empire* is the integration of past and present within the socialist community, that integration occurs at the expense of the image of the woman, who is defined as an objectified other. As a result, the two opposing orders associated with Fillimonov and the woman's present husband share the common status of the woman as object. *Man with a Movie Camera* celebrates the fusion of human activity and technology, with figures of women occupying a particularly strategic place as privileged signs of socialist utopia. But the female form also represents a resistance to this enthusiastic celebration of the fusion of cinematic and socialist vision.

I would like to return to *Man with a Movie Camera* for a moment, and to one image in particular that was not discussed in the previous chapter. In a continuation of the theme of superfluous (e.g., cosmetic) versus genuine labor, which is so important to the film, there appear several images of large, overweight women, dressed in exercise clothing, working out on various kinds of exercise equipment. Their appearance suggests another kind of resistance to technology. At other moments in the film, a resistance to the technological force of cinematic perception is suggested by the carefully shielded female face that turns away from the gaze of the camera, and by the abrupt, embarrassed departure of the woman caught by the camera as she awakens from a night spent on a park bench, her legs briefly fragmented and spied upon by the exuberant cameraman just before she awakens. In the images of these large women, however, the tension between technology and resistance to it is quite literally embodied in the figure of woman as an expanse of flesh. There is nothing in the gestures of the women to suggest discomfort with the camera, but rather it is the body itself that exists in opposition to the machine. Certainly, the rapid montage used here undercuts somewhat the impression of sheer corporeal abundance and fragments the body by juxtaposing it to other bodies that conform more to a traditional and, it is assumed, socialist ideal. These female bodies are meant to be humorous; they stand in sharp contrast to the athletic bodies engaged in sports to which they are compared. If the large female body is meant to be connoted as bourgeois, as are the images of women being beautified in a variety of ways, the connotation is somewhat less clear-cut. The clothing here is not decorative, and the pursuit of fitness, even if artificial, does not have quite the same negative connotations as the cosmetic industry does.[3]

The figure of woman in these images suggests a tension between the female body as flesh, as corporeal presence, as a quite literal excess, and the technological form that works that flesh into shape, whether in the literal form of the exercise machines which create the athletic body or in the figurative form of the cinema which idealizes it. To be sure, the idealized body is male as well as female. That is precisely the point: the unruly, resistant, recalcitrant female body threatens the ideal form, not only of sleek muscles and graceful movements, but of identity and sameness, of the body as machine. This enthusiastic representation of the fusion of technology and the cinema relies on a contrast between the functional "human" body and the feminine body ostensibly burdened by excess. This opposition, between the female body and the human body, is a remarkably emblematic representation of the contradictory relationship between Soviet film narrative and the woman question. Whether it be the disruptive female presence which hinders the growth of class solidarity in *Strike*, the inaccessibility of the woman to the realm of metaphoric representation in *Mother*, the containment of the woman within the boundaries of both the image and the past in *Fragment of an*

Empire, or the affirmation of maternity as an alternative to male hegemony in *Bed and Sofa,* the woman question echoes throughout Soviet film practice as a nagging reminder that the female body does not always fit neatly into patterns of narrative, cinematic or ideological opposition.

Notes

INTRODUCTION

1. Hence, *Fragment of an Empire* and *Man with a Movie Camera* would, in the name of socialist realism, be criticized as "formalist." See Denise Youngblood, *Soviet Cinema in the Silent Era, 1918–1935* (Ann Arbor: UMI Research Press, 1985), p. 204.
2. Laura Mulvey, "Visual Pleasure and Narrative Cinema," *Screen* 16, no. 3 (Autumn 1975): 11.
3. For an elaborate and detailed exploration of the classical Hollywood cinema as style and as institution, see David Bordwell, Janet Staiger, and Kristin Thompson, *The Classical Hollywood Cinema: Film Style and Mode of Production to 1960* (New York: Columbia University Press, 1985).
4. For a more extensive discussion of the issues in feminist film theory and criticism, see Judith Mayne, "Review Essay: Feminist Film Theory and Criticism," *Signs* 11, no. 1 (Autumn 1985): 81–100.
5. Kaja Silverman, "Lost Objects and Mistaken Subjects: Film Theory's Structuring Lack," *Wide Angle* 7, no. 1–2 (1985): 25.
6. For a discussion and overview of the woman question in the Soviet Union, see Mary Buckley, "Soviet Interpretations of the Woman Question," in Barbara Holland, ed., *Soviet Sisterhood: British Feminists on Women in the U.S.S.R.* (London: Fourth Estate, 1985), pp. 24–53.
7. Ernest Jones writes that Freud once said to Marie Bonaparte: "The great question that has never been answered and which I have not yet been able to answer, despite my thirty years of research into the feminine soul, is 'What does a woman want?'" See *Sigmund Freud: Life and Work*, vol. 2 (New York: Basic Books, 1955), p. 468.
8. Roland Barthes, "Writers, Intellectuals, Teachers," in *Image, Music, Text*, Stephen Heath, ed. & trans. (London: Fontana, 1977), p. 212.

9. André Bazin, *What is Cinema?* (Berkeley: University of California Press, 1967), Hugh Gray, ed. & trans. pp. 35, 36.
10. Jean-Louis Comolli, "Technique et Idéologie: Caméra, perspective, profondeur de champ," *Cahiers du cinéma,* no. 230 (July 1971): 51–57.
11. Marie-Claire Ropars, "Fonction de la métaphore dans *Octobre* d'Eisenstein," *Littérature,* no. 11 (October 1973): 126.
12. David Bordwell, *Narration in the Fiction Film* (Madison: University of Wisconsin Press, 1985), pp. 241, 262.
13. Olga Preobrazhenskaya's best-known film is *Women of Ryazan;* see Jay Leyda, *Kino: A History of the Russian and Soviet Film* (1960; rpt. New York: Collier, 1973), p. 231; and Youngblood, *Soviet Cinema in the Silent Era,* p. 150. On Esther Shub, see Vlada Petric, "Esther Shub: Cinema is My Life," and "Esther Shub's Unrealized Project," *Quarterly Review of Film Studies* 3, no. 4 (1978): 429–46.
14. Teresa DeLauretis, *Alice Doesn't: Feminism, Semiotics, Cinema* (Bloomington: Indiana University Press, 1984), p. 5.

CHAPTER ONE

1. Richard Taylor, *The Politics of the Soviet Cinema 1917–1929* (Cambridge: Cambridge University Press, 1979), p. 43.
2. See also Youngblood, *Soviet Cinema in the Silent Era.*
3. Bordwell, *Narration in the Fiction Film,* pp. 241–42.
4. Sheila Rowbotham, *Women, Resistance and Revolution* (1972; rpt. New York: Vintage, 1974), pp. 149–50.
5. For a discussion of RAPP, see Marc Slonim, *Soviet Russian Literature: Writers and Problems* (New York: Oxford University Press, 1964), p. 156.
6. For a discussion of the legal and civil status of women in Russia in the nineteenth century, see Linda Harriet Edmondson, *Feminism in Russia, 1900–1917* (London: Heinemann Educational Books, 1984), pp. 11–15.
7. Leyda, *Kino,* p. 132.
8. On *Strike,* see Eisenstein's 1925 essay "On the Question of a Materialist Approach to Form," in P. Adams Sitney, ed., Roberta Reeder, trans. *The Avant-Garde Film: A Reader of Theory and Criticism* (New York: New York University Press, 1978), pp. 17–18. On *Potemkin,* see Eisenstein's 1939 introduction to the screenplay, in *Potemkin* (New York: Simon & Schuster, 1968), pp. 7–21.

9. Dziga Vertov, *Kino-Eye: The Writings of Dziga Vertov,* Annette Michelson, ed. Kevin O'Brien, trans. (1926; rpt. Berkeley: University of California Press, 1984), p. 69.

10. Sergei Eisenstein, "Dickens, Griffith and the Film Today," Jay Leyda, trans. in *Film Form* (1949; rpt. Cleveland: World Publishing Company, 1957), p. 235.

11. Ibid., p. 234.

12. Vertov, *Kino-Eye,* p. 67.

13. For a discussion of the relationship between Soviet filmmakers and traditional modes of cinematic representation, see Noël Burch, "Film's Institutional Mode of Representation and the Soviet Response," *October,* no. 11 (1979): 77–96.

14. Responding to the argument concerning the career of Sergei Eisenstein, that in the 1920s Eisenstein was radical, only to become idealist in the 1930s and 1940s, Jacques Aumont writes that such an argument "dismisses the fact that this contradiction, this struggle between a conception of the conflict and a demand for unity, for organicism, is constant in Eisenstein." What Aumont says of Eisenstein's career is an appropriate reminder that similar struggles, with different terms, characterized many films of the 1920s. See *Montage Eisenstein,* Lee Hildreth, Constance Penley, and Andrew Ross, trans. (1979; rpt. Bloomington: Indiana University Press, 1987), p. 67.

15. V. I. Lenin, "L. N. Tolstoy," in *On Socialist Ideology and Culture* (Moscow: Progress Publishers, 1962), pp. 60, 61.

16. V. I. Lenin, *Collected Works* (London: Lawrence & Wishart, 1963–69), vol. 6.

17. Peter Reddaway, "Literature, the Arts and the Personality of Lenin," in Leonard Schapiro and Peter Reddaway, eds., *Lenin: The Man, the Theorist, the Leader* (New York: Praeger, 1967), p. 40.

18. Cited in Louis Fischer, *The Life of Lenin* (New York: Harper and Row, 1964), pp. 504–05.

19. For a discussion of the significance of Chernyshevsky's novel in relation to the development of feminism in Russia, see Richard Stites, *The Women's Liberation Movement in Russia* (Princeton: Princeton University Press, 1978), pp. 89–99.

20. For discussion of how the reputed romantic relationship between Lenin and Armand appears to have little basis in fact, see Stites, *The Women's Liberation Movement in Russia,* p. 324; and Bertram D. Wolfe, "Lenin and Inessa Armand," *Slavic Review* vol. 22 (1963): 96–114.

21. David Shub, *Lenin* (1948; rept. New York: Penguin, 1966),

p. 138. Wolfe, in "Lenin and Inessa Armand" (p. 98), reports that "Chernyshevsky's novel was the chief instrument of the conversion of Inessa to socialism."

22. Letter to Inessa Armand on January 24, 1915, in *The Emancipation of Women: From the Writings of V. I. Lenin* (New York: International Publishers, 1934), p. 40.

23. See Judith Mayne, *Private Novels, Public Films* (Athens: University of Georgia Press, 1988).

24. Cited in Leyda, *Kino,* p. 161.

25. Ibid., pp. 160–161.

26. See Edmondson, *Feminism in Russia, 1900–1917,* and Stites, *The Women's Liberation Movement in Russia.*

27. See Stites, *The Women's Liberation Movement in Russia,* p. 323.

28. See Beatrice Farnsworth, *Aleksandra Kollontai: Socialism, Feminism, and the Bolshevik Revolution* (Stanford: Stanford University Press, 1980), p. 85.

29. See Farnsworth, pp. 157–59 for a discussion of Kollontai, Lenin, and the Family Code.

30. Farnsworth, p. 291

31. See Cathy Porter, *Alexandra Kollontai: A Biography* (London: Virago, 1980), p. 351.

32. See Farnsworth, especially pp. 302–08; and Porter, pp. 239, 347–97.

33. Porter, p. 422.

34. Farnsworth, p. 348.

35. Ibid., p. 366.

36. Victor Shklovsky, "Art as Technique," in Lee T. Lemon and Marion J. Reis, ed., *Russian Formalist Criticism: Four Essays* (Lincoln: University of Nebraska Press, 1965), pp. 3–25. Speaking specifically of Eisenstein's theories of montage, Herbert Eagle notes that for Eisenstein, "the montage process is based on conflict, opposition, deautomatization in Sklovskij's terms." See "Russian Formalist Film Theory: An Introduction," in Herbert Eagle, ed., *Russian Formalist Film Theory* (Ann Arbor: Michigan Slavic Publications, 1981), p. 34.

37. V. I. Pudovkin, Ivor Montagu, ed. & trans. *Film Technique and Film Acting* (1949; rpt. New York: Grove Press, 1970), p. 262.

38. Sergei Eisenstein, "Word and Image," in Jay Leyda, ed. and trans., *Film Sense* (New York: Harcourt, Brace & World, 1942), p. 17.

39. Vertov, *Kino-Eye,* p. 66.

40. Pudovkin, *Film Technique and Film acting,* p. 261.

41. Lev Kuleshov, Ron Levaco, ed. & trans., *Kuleshov on Film* (Berkeley: University of California Press, 1974), p. 92.

42. Kuleshov, *Kuleshov on Film,* p. 53.

43. Villiers de l'Isle-Adam's 1886 novel *L'Eve Future,* about the creation of an ideal robotized woman, is particularly relevant to the emergence of the cinema as the embodiment of fantasy (the cinematic implications are particularly strong, given that Thomas A. Edison appears in the novel). See Annette Michelson, "On the Eve of the Future: The Reasonable Facsimile and the Philosophical Toy," *October,* no. 29 (Summer 1984): 3–20; and Raymond Bellour, Stanley E. Gray, trans. "Ideal Hadaly," *Camera Obscura* 15 (1986): 111–34. Lucy Fischer has analyzed how, in the magic films of Georges Méliès, the transformation of the female figure reveals persistent fantasies of fear and envy. See "The Lady Vanishes: Women, Magic and the Movies," in John Fell, ed., *Film Before Griffith* (Berkeley: University of California Press, 1983), pp. 339–54.

44. Vertov, *Kino-Eye,* p. 17. "Man" is meant here in the generic sense.

45. Eisenstein, "Through Theater to Cinema," in *Film Form,* p. 5.

46. Hélène Cixous, in Hélène Cixous and Catherine Clément, *The Newly Born Woman,* Betsy Wing, trans. (Minneapolis: University of Minnesota Press, 1986), p. 64.

47. See "The Structure of the Film," in *Film Form,* pp. 150–78.

48. As David Bordwell points out, however, there are several possible ways to read the final images of the sequence, and it seems highly unlikely that the woman's wound would come from a saber. "Rather than decide on a single construction," Bordwell says, "we should recognize that exactly this mixing of cues, this shaking of scenic components loose from a univocal fabula world, enables the narration to create an 'open' space from which can be selected maximally forceful images of brutality . . ." See *Narration in the Fiction Film,* pp. 246–47.

49. Roland Barthes, "The Third Meaning," in Stephen Heath, ed. & trans., *Image-Music-Text* (London: Fontana, 1977), pp. 54, 58–59.

50. See Roman Jakobson, "Two Aspects of Language and Two Types of Aphasic Disturbances," in *Selected Writings,* 2 vols. (The Hague: Mouton, 1971), vol. 2, pp. 239–59. For Jean Mitry, the example of the pince-nez illustrates the extent to which apparent cinematic metaphors are always metonymic and, therefore, not really possible in film. If the pince-nez has a metaphoric function, it is defined by the fact that the pince-nez has been defined previously as part of the doctor; that is, it is first and foremost metonymic.

See *Esthétique et psychologie du cinéma,* 2 vols. (Paris: Editions universitaires, 1963), vol. 1, pp.120–22. But as Linda Williams has pointed out, there is a normative tendency in Mitry's dismissal of cinematic metaphor; see *Figures of Desire: A Theory and Analysis of Surrealist Film* (Urbana: University of Illinois Press, 1981), pp. 59–61. It may well be more appropriate to describe the cinema, not as "non-metaphoric," but as both metaphoric and metonymic, its creation of figures revealing the extent to which the poles of metaphor and metonymy intersect.

51. Christian Metz, "Metaphor/Metonymy, or the Imaginary Referent," Celia Britton and Annwyl Williams, trans., in *The Imaginary Signifier* (Bloomington: Indiana University Press, 1982), p. 200.

52. Jack London, "The Unexpected," in *"Love of Life" and Other Stories* (New York: MacMillan, 1907), p. 141.

53. Ibid., p.165.

54. Leyda, *Kino,* p. 213. According to N. M. Lary, the source was a specific scene in Dostoevsky, in which "some Swiss townspeople exchange sentiments of love with a shepherd whom they are going to execute. Apparently, Shklovsky had no particular reason in mind when he used this episode out of Dostoevsky (and not uncharacteristically he even got his source wrong, indicating *The Demons* instead of *The Brothers Karamazov.*)" Lary cites his 1976 interview with Shklovsky, in which Shklovsky had no recollection as to the motivation for borrowing the scene from Dostoevsky. Lary suggests that perhaps the motivation had less to do with a specific scene that with "Dostoevsky's sense of the ambiguity of experience and of the hypocrisy of men." See *Dostoevsky and Soviet Film: Visions of Demonic Realism* (Ithaca: Cornell University Press, 1986), p. 39.

55. Marc Ferro, *Cinéma et histoire* (Paris: Denoël, 1977), pp. 111–12.

56. Noël Burch describes Kuleshov's films (*By the Law* as well as *The Death Ray* [1925] and *The Extraordinary Adventures of Mr. West in the Land of the Bolsheviks* [1924]) as evidence of the filmmaker's concern with "studying and appropriating the codes governing the major genres of the capitalist film industry." According to Burch, "[t]he guiding principle behind all these productions was that the institutional mode of representation, the genres and other coded systems founded upon it, offered ideal vehicles in the ideological struggle because of the privileged relationships which they already enjoyed with mass audiences." See "Film's Institutional Mode of Representation and the Soviet Response," p. 85.

57. For analyses of *October,* see Rosalind Krauss, "Montage 'October':

Dialectic of the Shot," *Artforum* 11, no. 5 (January 1973): 61–65; and Annette Michelson, "Camera Lucida/Camera Obscura," *Artforum* 11, no. 5 (January 1973): 30–37.

58. For discussions of the controversy about *October,* see Leyda, *Kino,* pp. 231–41; and Richard Taylor, *Film Propaganda: Soviet Russia and Nazi Germany* (New York: Barnes and Noble, 1979), chapter six.

59. The opening sequence is discussed in great detail in Pierre Sorlin and Marie-Claire Ropars, *Octobre: Ecriture et Idéologie* (Paris: Editions Albatross, 1976), pp. 11–85.

60. For a discussion of the "gods" sequence, see Noël Carroll, "For God and Country," *Artforum* 11, no. 5 (January 1973): 56–60; and Ropars, "Fonction de la métaphore dans *Octobre* d'Eisenstein," *Littérature,* no. 11 (October 1973): 109–28.

61. Sorlin and Ropars, *Octobre: Ecriture et Idéologie,* p. 147.

62. Ibid., p. 149; Sorlin makes this point.

63. Ropars argues that in *October,* there is a distinct difference in the way in which the bourgeoisie and the proletariat are designated in relationship to metaphor. In the realm of the proletariat, she says, metaphors emerge from relations of contiguity, whereas metaphors relevant to the bourgeoisie tend to be drawn from outside the immediacy of context. Ropars cites as evidence the process whereby a "metonymic representation of the people"— the young woman on the bridge and the slain Bolshevik— becomes a "symbolic and ideological representation which nonetheless remains more synecdochic than metaphoric." I am arguing, however, that the woman on the bridge does not belong to the same category of significance as the slain Bolshevik, for despite what Ropars says, the woman does not have the same relationship to the narrative context of the film as the young man. See "Fonction de la métaphore dans *Octobre* d'Eisenstein," *Littérature,* no. 11 (October 1973): 115.

64. Other female figures in *October* are cast by and large in functionary roles. These characterizations are not without interest. The women seen in a bread line, for example, are very much like the statues through which Eisenstein conveys the old, repressive order.

65. Andrew Britton, "Sexuality and Power or the Two Others," part 1, *Framework,* no. 6 (Autumn 1977): 10.

66. Ibid., p. 11.

67. This hypothesis is given extensive treatment by Dominique Fernandez, who analyzes Eisenstein's films as reenactments of the filmmaker's childhood traumas. Eisenstein's negative attitude

toward women is seen as the basis of a number of representations of women in his films. See Fernandez, *Eisenstein* (1975; rpt. Paris: Grasset, 1987).

68. Porter, *Alexandra Kollontai: A Biography*, p. 265.

69. Stites notes that there were more armed Bolshevik women involved in the October Revolution than there were members of the Women's Battalion. See *The Women's Liberation Movement in Russia*, p. 306.

70. Porter, *Alexandra Kollontai: A Biography*, p. 265.

71. Louise Bryant, *Six Red Months in Russia* (1918; rpt. Colombo, Sri Lanka: Young Socialist Publications, 1973), p. 143.

72. For discussions of the relationship between *Earth* and Stalin's agricultural policy, see Vance Kepley, *In the Service of the State: The Cinema of Alexander Dovzhenko* (Madison: University of Wisconsin Press, 1986), pp. 75–79; and Paul E. Burns, "Cultural Revolution, Collectivization, and Soviet Cinema: Eisenstein's *Old and New* and Dovzhenko's *Earth*," *Film and History* 2, no. 4 (1981): 84–96.

73. As Kepley points out, the contrast between the two dances—the "private, spontaneous celebration" signified by Vasyl's dance versus the "comic spectacle" of Khoma's parody—is further accentuated by the fact that Khoma dances in a graveyard, "suggesting that Khoma and the kulaks are doomed to obsolescence." See Kepley, *In the Service of the State*, p. 82.

74. Eisenstein, "Dickens, Griffith and the Film Today," in *Film Form*, p. 241. In a note to the essay, Eisenstein notes that Griffith edits two Whitman phrases, which are in fact twenty lines apart: "Out of the cradle endlessly rocking . . ." and " . . . Uniter of Here and Hereafter."

75. Ibid.

CHAPTER TWO

1. Eisenstein, "The Cinematographic Principle and the Ideogram," in *Film Form*, p. 37.

2. Pascal Bonitzer describes *Strike* in terms of spatial oppositions, with capitalists occupying an elevated space, the subproletarians occupying a subterranean space, and the working class occupying the surface. For Bonitzer, *Strike* is thus informed by what he calls "the victory of the surface," i.e., a destruction of the spatial polarity of high versus low. Central to Bonitzer's reading of the

film is the way in which the "underworld" mirrors the capitalists. Hence, Bonitzer argues that whatever decentering might occur in narrative and visual terms in *Strike,* the film is nonetheless "recentered" in the way that proletarian ideology emerges in mythic terms. See Bonitzer's "Le Système de *La Grève,*" *Cahiers du cinéma,* no. 226–227 (January–February 1971): 42–44. I suggest that if there is indeed a "recentering" in *Strike,* it has more to do with a notion of the public sphere as a brotherhood in which women function as a disruptive force.

3. For a discussion of Eisenstein's experience in the theater, see Marie Seton, *Sergei M. Eisenstein* (New York: Grove Press, 1960), pp. 56–72.

4. Eisenstein, "Montage of Attractions," in *Film Sense,* pp. 230–31.

5. Stephen Crofts, "Eisenstein and Ideology," *Framework,* no. 7–8 (Spring 1978): 14.

6. Clara Zetkin, "My Recollections of Lenin (An Interview on the Woman Question)," in *The Emancipation of Women: From the Writings of V. I. Lenin* (1934; rpt. New York: International Publishers, 1966), p. 115.

7. Annette Michelson, "Reading Eisenstein Reading *Capital,*" *October,* no. 2 (1976): 37. Eisenstein's criticisms of *Strike* are found in "On the Question of a Materialist Approach to Form," in *The Avant-Garde Film: A Reader of Theory and Criticism,* p. 34.

8. Eisenstein, "Notes for a Film of *Capital,*" Maciej Sliwowski, Jay Leyda, and Annette Michelson, trans. *October,* no. 2 (1978): 16.

9. Jakobson, "Two Aspects of Language and Two Types of Aphasic Disturbances," in *Selected Writings,* pp. 239–59. The operations of both metaphor and metonymy function to assign a totem status to the spies, according to Pascal Bonitzer; see "Le Système de *La Grève,*" p. 44.

10. Crofts, "Eisenstein and Ideology," p. 15.

CHAPTER THREE

1. See Richard Hare, *Maxim Gorky: Romantic Realist* (London and New York: Oxford University Press, 1962), p. 73.

2. Nathan Zarkhy, Introduction to *Two Russian Film Classics: "Mother" and "Earth"* (New York: Simon and Schuster, 1973), p. 8.

3. Ibid.

4. Ben Brewster has noted this privileged access, as well as the fact

that "the natural setting is never allowed to function within the context of verisimilitude . . ." "Pudovkin, Brecht, and *The Mother,*" lecture presented at the Center for 20th Century Studies, University of Wisconsin—Milwaukee, February 1977.

5. Ibid. Brewster notes that Pavel's reunion with his mother occurs through the killing of the father, and through the failure to get together with the woman revolutionary, since they miss each other during the escape at the prison.

6. Leyda, *Kino:* p. 207.

7. L. N. Tolstoy, *Resurrection* (1899; rpt. New York: New American Library, 1961), p. 80.

8. Richard Taylor, *Film Propaganda: Soviet Russia and Nazi Germany* (New York: Barnes and Noble, 1979), p. 87.

9. Alexandra Kollontai, "Women Workers Struggle for Their Rights" Celia Britton, trans. (1918; rpt. Bristol, England: Falling Wall Press, 1971), p. 16.

10. Kollontai, "Communism and the Family," in Alix Holt, ed., *Alexandra Kollontai: Selected Writings* (New York: Norton, 1977), p. 250.

11. See Youngblood, *Soviet Cinema in the Silent Era,* p. 88.

CHAPTER FOUR

1. Review of *Bed and Sofa* (n.a.), *Close Up,* no. 6 (December 1927): 69.

2. For discussions of the importance of the film's title, see Paul E. Burns, "An NEP Moscow Address: Abram Room's *Third Meshchanskaia (Bed and Sofa)* in Historical Context," *Film and History* 13, no. 4 (December 1982): 73–81; and Steven P. Hill, *"Bed and Sofa,"* *Film Heritage* 7, no. 1 (Fall 1971): 19.

3. Burns notes that the husband "is refurbishing a structure symbolic of the Old Regime, rather than working at one of the many new construction sites, just as in his private life he represents the carry-over of pre-revolutionary social attitudes." See "An NEP Moscow Address," p. 77.

4. See Eve Kosofsky Sedgwick, *Between Men: English Literature and Male Homosocial Desire* (New York: Columbia University Press, 1985), especially pp. 1–27.

5. Gayle Rubin's analysis of the function of the exchange of women in Lévi-Strauss's writings is extremely relevant in this context. See "The Traffic in Women: Notes on the 'Political Economy' of Sex," in Rayna R. Reiter, ed., *Toward an Anthropology of Women* (New York: Monthly Review Press, 1975), pp. 157–210.

6. Molly Haskell, *From Reverence to Rape* (New York: Holt, Rinehart and Winston, 1974), p. 320.

7. Beth Sullivan, "Bed and Sofa/Master of the House," *Women and Film*, no. 1 (1972): 23.

8. Kollontai, "Make Way for Winged Eros: A Letter to Working Youth" (1923), in Alix Holt, ed., *Alexandra Kollontai: Selected Writings*, p. 279.

9. Bryher was extremely critical of this resolution, calling it a "concession to popular ideas." See her *Film Problems of Soviet Russia* (Switzerland: Territet, 1929), pp. 74–75.

10. Mary Buckley, "Soviet Interpretations of the Woman Question," in Barbara Holland, ed., *Soviet Sisterhood* (London: Fourth Estate Limited, 1985), p. 34.

11. Burns, "An NEP Moscow Address," p. 78.

12. Kollontai, "The Labour of Women in the Revolution of the Economy" (1923), in *Alexandra Kollontai: Selected Writings*, p. 149.

13. Kollontai, "Vasilisa Malygina," Cathy Porter, trans., in *The Love of Worker Bees* (London: Virago Press, 1977), pp. 151–52.

CHAPTER FIVE

1. See Youngblood, *Soviet Cinema in the Silent Era*, pp. 208–09.

2. Oswell Blakeston, "Three More Russian Films," *Close Up* 6, no. 1 (January 1930): 32.

3. As Leyda points out, Lenin's complete works clearly have never been opened. See *Kino:* p. 258.

4. Ibid., p. 257.

5. Commenting on the argument between Fillimonov's ex-wife and her present husband, Blakeston offers another view: "This stuff dragged in to prove that it is the influence of the revolution, not the influence of the dream woman, which has changed the lovely Eisenstein type to the proletarian Menjou." See "Three More Russian Films," p. 33.

CHAPTER SIX

1. The classic statement of the position is Laura Mulvey's "Visual Pleasure and Narrative Cinema," *Screen* 16, no. 3 (Autumn 1975): 6–18.

2. See, for example, E. Ann Kaplan's discussion of the "avant-garde

theory film" in *Women and Film: Both Sides of the Camera* (New York: Methuen, 1983), pp. 142–70.

3. Roland Barthes, Richard Miller, trans. *S/Z* (1970; New York: Hill & Wang, 1974), pp. 3–4.

4. Eisenstein, "The Cinematographic Principle and the Ideogram," in *Film Form,* p. 43.

5. Michelson, "Introduction," *Kino-Eye: The Writings of Dziga Vertov,* p. xxxvii.

6. See Annette Michelson, "*The Man with a Movie Camera:* From Magician to Epistemologist," *Artforum* 10, no. 7 (March 1972): 60–72. For a detailed reading of *Man with a Movie Camera* in relation to ideology, aesthetics, and everyday life, see Vlada Petric, *Constructivism in Film: The Man with the Movie Camera* (Cambridge and London: Cambridge University Press, 1987).

7. See, for example, Gérard Leblanc, "Quelle avant-garde? Notes sur une pratique actuelle du cinéma militant," *Cinéthique,* no. 7–8 (n.d.): 72–92.

8. Alan Williams, "The Camera-Eye and the Film: Notes on Vertov's 'Formalism,'" *Wide Angle* 3, no. 3 (1979): 16.

9. Michelson, "Introduction," *Kino-Eye: The Writings of Dziga Vertov,* pp. xxxviv, xl.

10. Williams, "The Camera-Eye and the Film," p. 17.

11. Mulvey, "Visual Pleasure and Narrative Cinema."

12. See, for example, Lucy Fischer, "The Lady Vanishes: Women, Magic, and the Movies," *Film Quarterly* 33, no. 1 (Fall 1979): 30–40; Judith Mayne, "Der primitive Erzähler," *Frauen und Film,* no. 41 (1986): 4–16; and Linda Williams, "Film Body: An Implantation of Perversions," *Ciné-tracts* 3, no. 4 (Winter 1981): 19–35.

13. Vertov, "The Birth of Kino-Eye (1924)," in *Kino-Eye,* p. 42.

14. Vertov, "From Kino-Eye to Radio-Eye (1929)," in *Kino-Eye,* p. 88.

15. As Youri Tsyviane points out, a film poster is intercut with the initial images of the woman in the room, and the film being advertised is later revealed to be an "artistic drama," entitled *The Awakening of a Woman;* thus, says Tsyviane, *Man with a Movie Camera* is a similar awakening from "the bad dream of artistic cinema." See "*L'Homme à la caméra* de Dziga Vertov en tant que texte constructiviste," *Revue du cinéma,* no. 351 (June 1980): 124–25.

16. Vlada Petric discusses the "awakening" sequence in detail; see *Constructivism in Film,* pp. 164–176. Stephen Crofts and Olivia Rose suggest that it is *only* the woman's class status that is

significant; hence, they write that "her class position is defined
. . . by her wearing styled lingerie (hence the montage's stress on
her bra and slip) . . ." See "An Essay Towards *Man with a Movie
Camera*," *Screen* 18, no. 1 (Spring 1977): 36. The authors emphasize throughout their essay that the film's "open-ended structure
neither dictates a single reading nor proposes indiscriminate
choices within a range of possible readings, but rather directs the
spectator towards readings promoting ideological awareness" (p.
34). Unfortunately, the authors' notion of ideological awareness
does not seem to extend to gender, except as a reflection of class.

17. Seth Feldman, "Cinema Weekly and Cinema Truth: Dziga Vertov and the Leninist Proportion," *Sight and Sound* 43 (Winter
1973–74): 35.

18. Williams, "The Camera-Eye and the Film," p. 17.

19. Crofts and Rose, "An Essay Towards *Man with a Movie Camera*,
p. 38.

AFTERWORD

1. Michèle Lagny, Marie-Claire Ropars, and Pierre Sorlin, *La Révolution Figurée: Film, histoire, politique* (Paris: Editions Albatros,
1979), p. 1. My translation.

2. See Dana Polan, " 'Desire Shifts the Differance': Figural Poetics
and Figural Politics in the Film Theory of Marie-Claire Ropars,"
Camera Obscura, no. 12 (1984): 67–85.

3. Crofts and Rose, however, read the function of the large women
purely in terms of class contrast: "The film sets up a manifest
contrast . . . between the apparent vanity and self-consciousness
of the new bourgeoisie and the 'natural' response of the proletariat before the camera. . . . The same vanity marks the
'weightwatchers'. . . . Counterposing the excess consumption of
the 'weightwatchers' is the physical culture which was promoted
at the time and which is used to satirize it. The 'weightwatchers'
are intercut, for instance, with shotputters whose aim seems,
across the cuts, to be directed at the formers' heads." See "An
Essay Towards *Man with a Movie Camera*," p. 37. As I've noted
elsewhere, this detailed analysis marginalizes any questions—
such as those concerning gender—that might put into question
the political efficacy of the film.

Index

Abortion, 110, 112, 122–26
Activity, versus passivity, 31–34, 175
Adaptation, novel to film, 17, 93
Ambiguity: and *écriture*, 8–10; and figural representation, 186–87; and metaphor, 109; and montage, 119, 145, 148; and point of view, 164, 165; and representations of women, 34, 43, 86, 90, 135, 145, 165, 188
Armand, Inessa, 23, 24
Aumont, Jacques, 195n. 14
Avant-garde cinema, 155, 157, 185

Barthes, Roland, 5, 39, 155
Bazin, André, 5, 6, 8, 9
Bed and Sofa (Abram Room), 10, 110–29, 130, 185, 188, 189, 192
Bellour, Raymond, 197n. 43
Blakeston, Oswell, 203n. 5
Bolsheviks, 13, 27, 28, 50–56
Bonitzer, Pascal, 200n. 2, 201n. 9
Bordwell, David, 7, 8, 9, 13, 193n. 3, 197n. 48
Brewster, Ben, 202nn. 4, 5
British Sounds (Jean-Luc Godard), 157
Britton, Andrew, 55
Bryant, Louise, 57
Bryher, 203n. 9

Buckley, Mary, 193n. 6
Burch, Noël, 195n. 13, 198n. 56
Burns, Paul E., 125, 200n. 72, 202n. 3
By the Law (Lev Kuleshov), 43–50

Cahiers du cinéma, 186
Capitalism, 18, 19, 66, 67, 78, 90, 179
Capital (Karl Marx), 88
Chernyshevsky, Nikolai, 22, 23, 24, 49
Cinéthique, 186
Civil War, 132
Cixous, Hélène, 33
Classical Hollywood cinema, 2–5, 165
Class struggle, 9, 12, 14, 35, 45, 53, 60, 63–64, 68, 104, 142, 177, 181, 189
Close Up, 111
Closure, 161
Communist Party, 28, 29
Comolli, Jean-Louis, 6, 8
Crofts, Stephen, 84, 90, 179, 204n. 16, 205n. 3

Deep focus, 6
Defamiliarization, 68–69, 70, 188. See also *Priem ostranenie*
DeLauretis, Teresa, 10
Displaced vision, 75, 83, 130

Domesticity, 75, 78, 80, 88, 94, 102, 110, 112–22, 123, 126–29, 130, 147. *See also* Private and public spheres; Woman question
Dostoevsky, Fyodor, 47, 48, 49, 103
Dovzhenko, Alexander, 61. See also *Earth*

Eagle, Herbert, 196n. 36
Earth (Alexander Dovzhenko), 57–63
Ecriture, in cinema, 9, 39, 52, 85, 156, 178, 189
Edmondson, Linda Harriet, 194n. 6
Eisenstein, Sergei, 17, 18, 19, 20, 30, 33, 54, 56, 61, 63, 65, 68, 71, 79, 83, 86, 88, 89, 156, 157, 186, 200n. 74. See also *October; Potemkin; Strike*
Ermler, Friedrich. See *Fragment of an Empire*

Farnsworth, Beatrice, 29
February Revolution, 50
Feldman, Seth, 176
Feminism, 184, 187; in the Soviet Union, 27, 28, 30, 125, 146. *See also* Kollontai, Alexandra; Woman question
Feminist film theory, 1–3
Feminist theory and criticism, 10, 155, 165; and textual analysis, 11. *See also* Gender; Woman question
Fernandez, Dominique, 199n. 67
Figures, in cinema, 26, 42, 131, 181, 186–87, 189. *See also* Metaphor; Montage
Fischer, Lucy, 197n. 43
Formalism, 156, 186

Fragment of an Empire (Friedrich Ermler), 10, 130–53, 188, 190, 191
Freud, Sigmund, 4

Gay male sexuality, 55
Gender, 1, 9, 11, 21, 49, 60, 66, 145, 146, 152, 154–56, 158, 165, 176, 182, 184, 185, 188. *See also* Feminism; Sexual politics; Woman question
Gish, Lillian, 61–62
Godard, Jean-Luc, 157
Gorky, Maxim, 91–93, 102, 103, 108. See also *Mother*
Griffith, D. W., 18, 61, 63. See also *Intolerance*
Groupe Dziga Vertov, 157

Haskell, Molly, 121

Ideology, 7, 12, 15, 16, 25, 131, 151, 159
Intolerance (D. W. Griffith), 61–63

Jakobson, Roman, 40. *See also* Metaphor and metonymy

Kepley, Vance, 200nn. 72, 73
Kerensky, Alexander, 27, 51
Kollontai, Alexandra, 28, 29, 105, 106, 121–22, 125, 126–29. See also *Vasilisa Malygina*
Kuleshov, Lev, 32, 33, 43. See also *By the Law*

Lagny, Michèle, 186
La Révolution figurée: film, histoire, politique (Michèle Lagny, Marie-Claire Ropars, and Pierre Sorlin), 186–87
Lary, N. M., 198n. 54
Leninist Proportion, 25

Lenin, V. I., 19, 21, 22, 24, 25, 28, 49, 56, 87, 88, 147
Lesbianism, 53, 55
Leyda, Jay, 13, 16, 147
London, Jack, 43, 47, 49, 93, 103. See also By the Law
Luttes en Italie (Groupe Dziga Vertov), 157

Male and female relationships, 110, 111, 114, 128, 129, 152, 153, 164, 165, 175, 177, 181. See also Gender; Marriage; Sexual politics
Male bonding, 35, 37, 55, 120–22, 140, 145–46
Man with a Movie Camera (Dziga Vertov), 154–83, 188, 190
Marriage, 110, 180
Marxism, 4, 6, 29, 83, 157; and psychoanalysis, 5, 27
May 1968, 157
Meta-narrative, 162
Metaphor, 40, 63, 68, 96, 106–9, 110, 128, 129, 137, 139, 141, 142, 189; and metonymy, 40–42, 89–90, 107–8. See also Montage
Metz, Christian, 40, 41
Michelson, Annette, 88, 157, 164, 165, 197n. 43
Mitry, Jean, 197n. 50
Montage, 12, 14, 17–20, 30–34; and abstraction, 40–43, 137; and activity versus passivity, 34–40; alternating, 75, 76, 78, 89, 167, 168; and ambiguity, 8; of attractions, 84; in Bed and Sofa (Abram Room), 111, 118; and binary opposition, 33; and classical film theory, 5–6; in Earth (Alexander Dovzhenko), 60–63; in Fragment of an Empire

(Friedrich Ermler), 135–42, 145, 147; and D. W. Griffith, 18; in Man with a Movie Camera (Dziga Vertov), 154, 166–75, 180, 191; in Mother (V. I. Pudovkin), 94, 106–9; in October (Sergei Eisenstein), 50–57; in Potemkin (Sergei Eisenstein), 34–43; in Strike (Sergei Eisenstein), 66, 68, 84–87, 89–90. See also Metaphor; Narration
Mother (V. I. Pudovkin), 91–109, 110, 128, 129, 130, 140, 184–85, 188, 189, 191
Mulvey, Laura, 2

Narration, 131, 139, 143, 162, 163. See also Montage; Point of view
Nature, 106–9, 128, 129, 130, 154
NEP (New Economic Policy), 27, 28, 58, 127

October Revolution (1917), 27, 28, 50
October (Sergei Eisenstein), 6, 50–57, 58, 65, 79, 186
Octobre: Ecriture et idéologie (Michèle Lagny, Marie-Claire Ropars, and Pierre Sorlin), 186
Oedipal scenarios, in narrative, 104, 109, 140

Petric, Vlada, 194n. 13, 204nn. 6, 16
Point of view, 144, 164, 165. See also Narration
Porter, Cathy, 56
Potemkin (Sergei Eisenstein), 13, 14, 18, 34–43, 50, 59, 62, 65
Pravda (Jean-Luc Godard), 157
Preobrazhenskaya, Olga, 10

Priem ostranenie ("the device of making strange"), 30, 68. *See also* Defamiliarization
Private and public spheres, 14, 23, 25, 26, 45, 49, 78, 80, 85–87, 94, 97, 103, 111–16, 126–29, 133, 141, 151, 154, 175, 176, 190. *See also* Domesticity
Psychoanalysis, 4; and Marxism, 5, 27
Pudovkin, V. I., 20, 30, 32, 68. See also *Mother*

RAPP (Russian Association of Proletarian Writers), 14
Realism, 19. *See also* Socialist realism
Religion, 35, 51, 59, 60, 92, 109
Resurrection (L. N. Tolstoy), 102–3
Ropars, Marie-Claire, 6, 186, 199n. 63
Room, Abram. See *Bed and Sofa*
Rose, Olivia, 179, 204n. 16, 205n. 3
Rowbotham, Sheila, 14
Rubin, Gayle, 202n. 5
Russian Formalism, 30, 68. *See also* Defamiliarization

Sedgwick, Eve Kosofsky, 120
Sexual politics, 1, 22, 23, 112, 126, 152, 155, 165, 184, 188. *See also* Feminism; Gender
Shklovsky, Victor, 47
Shub, Esther, 10
Silverman, Kaja, 3
Slonim, Marc, 194n. 5
Socialism, 12–14, 23, 26, 27, 29, 57, 66, 67, 70, 92, 104, 112, 139, 140, 143, 146, 148, 151, 153, 156, 157, 163, 179, 180
Socialist realism, 16, 66, 91, 187
Sorlin, Pierre, 51, 52, 53, 186

Spectatorship, 3, 71, 85, 86, 100–102, 115, 119, 130, 133, 153, 162
Staiger, Janet, 193n. 3
Stalin, Josef, 28, 58
Stites, Richard, 195nn. 19, 20, 200n. 69
Strike (Sergei Eisenstein), 18, 65–90, 91, 92–93, 109, 110, 130, 161, 188, 189, 191
Structuralism, 11
Sullivan, Beth, 121
Svilova, Elizaveta, 166

Taylor, Richard, 13, 103
Technology, 161, 190, 191
Tel Quel, 6
Textual analysis, 11
Thompson, Kristin, 193n. 3
Tolstoy, L. N., 21, 22, 56. See also *Resurrection*
Tsyviane, Youri, 204n. 15
Turgenev, Ivan, 16

Utopianism, 155, 158, 163, 164, 176, 179, 181, 187, 190

Vasilisa Malygina (Alexandra Kollontai), 126–29
Vertov, Dziga, 17, 18, 19, 20, 25, 33, 71, 186. See also *Man with a Movie Camera*
Villiers de l'Isle Adam, 197n. 43
Voyeurism, 83, 85, 158, 169, 170

What Is To Be Done? (Nikolai Cherneshevsky), 22, 23
What Is To Be Done? (V. I. Lenin), 22
Whitman, Walt, 61
Williams, Alan, 162, 164, 165, 178
Williams, Linda, 198n. 50
Wolfe, Bertram D., 195n. 20, 195n. 21

Woman question: and ambiguity, 9–10, 188; and binary opposition, 155, 192; and cinematic *écriture*, 154, 156, 189; and Marxism, 29; and Marxism and psychoanalysis, 4–5; and narrative, 15, 30, 64, 146, 158; and socialism, 14, 26, 142, 146; and urban vs. rural Russia, 29. *See also* Feminism; Sexual politics

Women's battalion, 53, 55, 56, 65

Youngblood, Denise, 193n. 1, 194n. 13

Zarkhy, Nathan, 92
Zetkin, Clara, 87
Zhdanov, Andrei, 16. *See also* Socialist realism